True Crime Stories

12 Shocking True Crime Murder Cases

True Crime Anthology Vol.2

By
Jack Rosewood
&
Rebecca Lo

Copyright © 2016 by Wiq Media

ALL RIGHTS RESERVED

No part of this book may be reproduced, stored in a retrieval system, or transmitted in any form or by any means, electronic, mechanical, photocopying, recording, scanning, or otherwise, without the prior written permission of the publisher.

ISBN-13: 978-1535271707

DISCLAIMER:

This crime anthology biography includes quotes from those closely involved in the twelve cases examined, and it is not the author's intention to defame or intentionally hurt anyone involved. The interpretation of the events leading up to these crimes are the author's as a result of researching the true crime murders. Any comments made about the psychopathic or sociopathic behavior of criminals involved in any of these cases are the sole opinion and responsibility of the person quoted.

Free Bonus!

Get two free books when you sign up to my VIP newsletter at www.jackrosewood.com
150 interesting trivia about serial killers
and the story of serial killer Herbert Mullin.

Contents

Introduction 1

CHAPTER 1: Murder in the French Alps – Iqbal Al-Hilli and her Family 3

    From Scenic Views to Crime Scene 3

    A Puzzle with Too Many Angles 5

    Saad Al-Hilli 5

    Sylvain Mollier 6

    The Work of a Serial Killer? 6

    Mystery Motorcyclist 7

    The Legionnaire 7

    Iqbal Al-Hilli 7

    A Secret Husband? 8

    Death by Coincidence 9

    Murder Unsolved 10

CHAPTER 2: The Villisca Axe Murders 13

    The Moore's 13

    A Gruesome Scene 14

    Who Were the Suspects? 17

Fourteen Witnesses Called to Coroner's Inquest............. 23

Deathbed and Jailhouse Confessions................................ 25

CHAPTER 3: The Disappearance of Stacy Peterson and Christie Marie Cales 28

The Troubled Life of Stacy... 28

Gone Without a Trace 30

Morphey's Story... 31

Kathleen Savio... 34

Another Wife Murdered? The Trial of Drew Peterson 36

Disappearance of Her Mother—Christie Marie Cales 37

CHAPTER 4: Lucia de Berk – Angel of Death? 39

Accused of Seven Cases of Murder and Three Cases of Attempted Murder 39

The Trial and Sentencing... 40

Doubts Emerge.. 42

Reopening of the Case 44

Justice Miscarried.. 45

CHAPTER 5: The Richardson Murders in Canada 47

The Discovery of the Crime Scene..................................... 47

A Shocking Suspect.. 48

Steinke Goes on Trial 50

A Lethal Romance 53

The Aftermath 55

CHAPTER 6: The Good Hart Murders 56

Family on Vacation 56

A Horrific Crime Scene.. 57

Evidence and Theories.. 59

The Suspects 60

Joseph R. Scolaro – Embezzler?... 67

Nothing Resolved….Yet 70

CHAPTER 7: Beslanowitch – The Murder of a Teen Prostitute 71

The Life of Krystal Beslanowitch.. 72

Cold on the River Bank 73

Reopening of the Case.. 74

DNA Points the Finger 75

Simpson's History – It Wasn't His First Murder...................... 76

CHAPTER 8: Murder or Accident? 78

Sherri Miller and Pam Jackson Disappear 78

A False Accusation.. 81

Skeletons in the Studebaker... 83

CHAPTER 9: When Suicide is Murder 85

- The Death of Pamela Shelly 85
- Television Steps In 88
- Ronnie Hendrick 90

CHAPTER 10: Snatched From the Snow 92

- The Disappearance of Maria Ridulph 92
- A Tragic Discovery 94
- Prime Suspect Right From the Start – Was Tessier Johnny? 95
- A Mother's Deathbed Confession 97
- A Long-Awaited Trial 99

CHAPTER 11: Captive for 24 Years – the Joseph Fritzl Case 100

- An Incestuous Situation 100
- A Visit to the Hospital Invokes Suspicion 102
- The Trial of Josef Fritzl 103
- The Psychological Scars and Fighting Back to Normality 104

CHAPTER 12: A Controversial Case of Police Misconduct – Or Was it Murder By Cop? 106

- Nizah Morris Left Lying in the Street 106
- Police Request a Second Opinion 108

The Investigation into the Officers 110
Police Advisory Commission Called In 110
Something Good from Something Bad 111

A Note From The Author 123

Introduction

Murder happens anywhere, at any time, and the rates of murder are increasing as is the size of the population around the world. Even an economic crisis can trigger an outbreak of sorts of murders. But there are always certain cases that stay in the recesses of your mind, even after years have passed. Why you remember them may depend on the individual case and whether or not you feel some kind of affinity with the victim. Others may stay in your memory because they are so horrific that you just can't forget about them. One thing's for sure—while the victim is being remembered, they are being honored in some small way. Remembering those who have been lost, helps to keep them alive, even if it is just in our memories.

There are twelve cases contained in this book. They range from multiple murders to mistaken identity crimes, as being accused and charged of a murder you didn't commit can also affect you for the rest of your life. There is a chapter on Josef Fritzl, the father who kept his daughter captive for twenty-four years, and the suicide that was found to be a homicide, thanks in part to a popular television program. An alleged angel of death, family murders, police misconduct, and the taking of a child—they are all stories that need to be remembered.

Some of these cases go back a long way, with one being the oldest cold case ever solved. Can you guess what it might be? Fifty years is a long time to wait to see justice done. Or was it? Twists, turns, puzzles, and psychopathy are all the makings of most of these murder cases. From the youngest victim to the youngest perpetrator, each chapter will draw you further into the history of these horrific crimes.

CHAPTER 1:
Murder in the French Alps – Iqbal Al-Hilli and her Family

The murders of three family members and what appeared to be a random cyclist, as well as the wounding of two children, created shockwaves around the world. The nationalities of the victims, the remoteness of the attack, and the fact that two little girls were left to hide amongst the dead, brought law agencies around the world into the investigation. There were so many questions that needed to be answered—why them? How did they know they would be there? Was the cyclist involved? Was it an international hit? And was there a lot more to the story than anyone had realized?

From Scenic Views to Crime Scene

The French Alps is perhaps one of the most beautiful locations in the world and is a popular destination for vacationers. It is no wonder that Iqbal Al-Hilli, her husband Saad, their two daughters, and her elderly mother Suhaila Al-Allaf too decided to choose the Alps for their family vacation. What would ensue, however, would dramatically alter the pristine landscape that was to become one of absolute horror on September 5, 2012.

On a remote scenic vista near historic Lake Annecy sat the BMW the family was using for their trip. Inside the car were the bodies of Iqbal, Saad, and Suhaila, all of whom had been shot. One of their daughters was found outside the car. The seven year old who had been shot in the shoulder and also had a wound to the head. At the time of the discovery, nobody was aware that there was another young daughter. She was hiding beneath her mother's legs in the back of the car and remained hidden for some eight hours, even while the local police were on the scene, until she was finally discovered unhurt.

Further along the road a short distance lay the body of a cyclist, Frenchman Sylvain Mollier. He had reportedly been shot seven times, though nobody had a clue why or how he was tied in with the murdered family. Each of the victims inside the car had been shot twice in the head, and evidence at the scene showed that twenty-five shots in total were fired. The engine of the car was still running when discovered, and the car had been shifted into reverse, with the back wheels spinning in the loose sandy gravel.

A Puzzle with Too Many Angles

Initially, the case was handled by the local police, called the Gendarme, and then the National Gendarme joined in. There were so many angles to the tragedy that it was never going to be an easy one to solve. From the nationalities of the victims to their families, their lines of work, and links to a Middle East dictator, there were so many possible motives that eventually France and Britain created a joint investigation team to investigate.

Saad Al-Hilli

One of the first leads investigated was the background of Saad Al-Hilli. Originally from Iraq, Saad had once worked as an engineer on what were considered to be sensitive topics in Iraq, and he subsequently was employed in the nuclear and satellite technology industry in England. Satellites, nuclear technology, and ties with Iraq alone were enough to consider the murders an act of assassination with Saad being the main target.

There were also suspicious circumstances surrounding the family of Saad, namely his father and his brother Zaid. There had been a claim that £840,000 had been placed in a Swiss bank account in Saad's father's name by the regime of Saddam Hussein. There were even reports leaked that showed Saad may have had access to Saddam Hussein's bank accounts.

Could the murders have been a contract hit related to the dictator?

To further add fuel to the theory of a family-related hit, his brother Zaid came under investigation due to a feud regarding a family inheritance. Zaid was eventually arrested in June 2013, but was subsequently released due to a lack of evidence, despite the suggestion that he tried to commit fraud by altering his father's will. However, suspicion always remained that he may have had a part to play in the murders.

Sylvain Mollier

Was Sylvain the innocent cyclist who was in the wrong place at the wrong time? Or was he the intended target and the family were the ones caught in the crossfire? Similar to Saad, Sylvain had also worked in the nuclear industry, and this was considered a possible lead. However, it was later substantiated that he was simply a welder and had no access to any delicate nuclear information, so this was later deemed unlikely to be the reason behind the murders. It seemed he really was just in the wrong place at the wrong time.

The Work of a Serial Killer?

This was perhaps one of the more far-fetched theories, with very little data to back it up. The detectives surmised that the murders were committed by a psychopath acting alone who perhaps had a dislike of tourists. This theory came about because of the similarities with a previous murder of a tourist in July 2012. There was never any real movement on this lead, and it was considered by most to be inconclusive.

Mystery Motorcyclist

A man riding a motorcycle was seen in the vicinity of the crime, but his identity was unknown. It wasn't until 2015 that the man in question was located by the police, and he was completely ruled out. He had simply been an innocent man out riding a motorcycle.

The Legionnaire

Patrice Menegaldo was an ex-soldier of the French Foreign Legion who found himself on the suspect list. He subsequently committed suicide, though the reason behind this is not clear. It is also not clear as to why he was ever considered a suspect, and despite the State Prosecutor at the time stating he was, the police denied he was ever considered a primary suspect.

Iqbal Al-Hilli

Initially the investigation focused on the background of her husband Saad and his potential links to both the nuclear industry and Saddam Hussein. Her background had seemed fairly straightforward, or so the investigators thought. However, it would later come out that she had a secret that very few people knew about, and this would lead to a further coincidental death and conspiracy.

A Secret Husband?

Before her marriage to Saad, Iqbal had once been married to an American gentleman named Jim Thompson. What had appeared to be simply a marriage of convenience to enable Iqbal to get her U.S. Green Card was perhaps more than anyone realized.

During her time in the U.S., Iqbal went by the name of Kelly, and upon meeting ex-cop Jim in 1999, he agreed to help her out by marrying her so that she could live and work there. The marriage was said to be platonic yet very caring. However, Iqbal discovered that her dentistry qualifications weren't accepted by the U.S. and ended the marriage just months later. Jim reluctantly drove her to the airport and said goodbye.

Her next contact with Jim was in 2003, when she declared she had fallen in love with another man, Saad, and she needed a divorce. Jim happily granted her the divorce, and she went on to marry the man she would later die with. But the story between Iqbal and Jim didn't end there.

Jim's sister Judy Weatherly would later state that Jim and Iqbal had stayed in touch throughout the nine years she was married to Saad. Regular emails went back and forth, and Iqbal's family knew nothing about it at all. They didn't even know she had once been married to Jim. There has even been suggestion that the divorce was never legalized, which would mean Iqbal had entered her marriage to Saad as a bigamist. So what was the importance of this secret relationship in relation to the murders? Here's where it gets even more bizarre and interesting.

Death by Coincidence

On exactly the same day that Iqbal and her family were slaughtered in the French Alps, her former husband Jim died at the wheel of his car, presumably from a heart attack. This extraordinary coincidence would lead the French investigators to question whether or not the deaths were related in some way. Jim may have been sixty years and had a history of high blood pressure, but the timing of his death seemed too much of a freak occurrence, considering what had happened to his ex-wife at that same point in time.

To further add to the speculation, he had allegedly called his sister Judith two weeks before his death and instructed her that if anything happened to him she was to go through his room, as there was something there that would be surprising. Judith followed through with his wishes, but the only thing she found was a box full of photos and information about his marriage to Iqbal. It seemed he clearly wanted people to know they had been married, but for what reason? Was he trying to say he had been forewarned or knew he was at risk of being killed?

The death of Jim became increasingly important to the French authorities, who started to question whether he had also been murdered due to something between him and Iqbal. The most likely scenario, according to the authorities, was that he had been poisoned, which would mimic a heart attack. They set about requesting an exhumation to test for the presence of poisons, but Judith would not allow it. The FBI also supported the request for an exhumation, but the American authorities refused, believing there were not sufficient grounds to commit such an act. As recent as 2015, the FBI has considered making a further request for the exhumation to take place, and questions are still not answered.

Murder Unsolved

To date, there has been no further progress in identifying the motive or the perpetrator of the tragic murders of the Al-Hilli family and the cyclist, Sylvain Mollier. Though there have been a number of theories and leads, they veer off in so many directions that it has proven impossible so far to narrow them down to one plausible suspect. Did Saddam Hussein's regime put a contract on Saad's head because he had accessed bank accounts he shouldn't have? Or did he have too much information regarding satellites and nuclear technologies in the Middle East?

Did Saad's brother Zaid have his own relatives executed over an inheritance? Or had he been stealing money from the family account and felt the need to remove any potential possibility of being discovered? After all, family feuds can often lead to violence. But to kill your own brother, his wife, her mother, and leave the two little girls orphans is a pretty big stretch. Not to mention the poor cyclist who just happened to come along at the wrong time.

Another thing to consider is that the girls were not killed. If it was a contract hit, why would they have left living witnesses? Sure, the girls were only young, but who knows what they may have seen, heard or experienced? The killer or killers had time to shoot each victim in the head twice, yet only one of the girls had injuries—a bullet to the shoulder and a head injury from being pistol-whipped. It's true that the youngest of the girls was hiding underneath the legs of her dead mother, but an assassin that knows who the family is and where they are going to be at that present moment in time would surely know there were two children also traveling in the car. Why were they spared? A heartless, psychopathic killer isn't going to worry about sparing the children—they simply wouldn't care.

Finally, strong consideration should be given to the possibility of Jim, Iqbal's first husband, having been murdered on the very same day. Sure, coincidences do occur, but this one is just so bizarre that it is too good to be true. What did he know? Had

Iqbal been confiding even more secrets to Jim? Why did he mention the possibility of something happening to him just weeks before he died? Unfortunately, there have been many questions and few answers in this case, and at this point in time they are no closer to solving it. The authorities involved in this case still hope for that major breakthrough that will put an end to this terrible mystery.

CHAPTER 2:
The Villisca Axe Murders

In 1912, Villisca was a small Midwestern town in Iowa with a population of just 2,500. Despite its size, it was a busy little town with trains coming and going every day, businesses up and down the streets, and it was home to the first publicly funded armory in the whole state. For many, the name 'Villisca' meant 'pleasant view' or 'pretty place'. But regardless of the business successes and the beauty of the town, its history would be forever marred by one single event—the brutal and horrifying murder of eight people in one house, on one night, with an axe.

The Moore's

The Moore family was well liked in the community, and their affluence was well known. The members of the family were Josiah, who was 43 at the time, his wife Sarah, aged 39, and their children, Herman Montgomery, aged 11, Mary Katherine, 10, Arthur Boyd, 7, and Paul Vernon, 5. They were regular church attendees, and on the evening of June 9, 1912, the children had been participating in the Presbyterian Church's

13

Children's Day Program. This program lasted until 9:30 p.m., and the Moore family invited two young girls, Ina Mae Stillinger, aged 8, and her sister Lena Gertrude, who was 12 years old, to stay the night in their home. All walked back to the home of the Moores, arriving somewhere between 9:45 to 10 p.m. No one is sure what time the family and their guests retired to bed that evening, or what if anything was amiss in the house when they got home. What is known, however, is that what did occur during the night in that house would become legendary, for all the wrong reasons.

A Gruesome Scene

On the morning of June 10, the next door neighbor, Mary Peckham, found it strange that the family next door was not up and about at 7 a.m. as they usually were. She was used to hearing and seeing the family members as they started their morning chores, but they hadn't appeared, and the curtains were all closed. Mary decided to check on the family and went and knocked on the door, but nobody responded. She tried to open the door, but it was still locked. Fearing something was very wrong, she called Josiah's brother Ross to investigate. Oddly, she first let the Moore's chickens out of their coop—goodness knows why.

Ross arrived at the house, and like Mary he knocked on the door, shouting out in the hopes that someone inside would hear him. On receiving no response, he proceeded to unlock the door with his copy of the key to the house. Mary waited anxiously on the porch as Ross entered the house and made his way into the guest bedroom. The scene that greeted him was horrific—the bodies of the Stillinger sisters dead in the bed. Moore instructed Mary to call the local officer, Hank Horton, who arrived within a short period of time. It was Horton who further investigated the rest of the house, finding body after body of the Moore family, all with horrific head wounds. In the guest room where the bodies of the Stillinger sisters lay was a bloodied axe, and that was immediately identified as the murder weapon.

Though the injuries to each of the victims were gruesome, it was Josiah who seemed to have been dealt the most vicious blows. Unlike the others who had been bludgeoned to death with the blunt end of the axe, it was the sharp end that had been used on Josiah. In fact, his wounds were so horrific that his eyes were missing in his cut-up face. Gouge marks in the ceilings of the bedrooms had been created by the swinging of the axe; in some cases, these gouges were in the center of the room, not near the beds, and it was surmised that the killer must have been in some sort of wild frenzy, swinging the axe triumphantly after each kill.

The pillows on the beds were soaked in blood and spattered with brain matter. By the time the first doctor entered the house, the blood had congealed into a jelly, and clots were noticeable, and this indicated they had been killed somewhere shortly after midnight. Each of the victims had their faces covered with their bedclothes, and all lay in their beds as though they had been killed while sleeping, except for Lena Stillinger. Her body showed defensive wounds, suggesting she had tried to fight off the attacker. Her nightgown had been pushed up and her underwear removed, and her body had been posed in a sexual manner. Naturally consideration was given to the possibility she had been sexually assaulted or raped, but this was never determined without a doubt.

There were other strange things about the crime scene that made no sense at all. Although it is normal to pull the curtains closed on the windows, those which did not have curtains were covered with clothing that had belonged to the victims. Every mirror in the house had also been covered, which was truly bizarre. At the foot of Josiah and Sarah's bed sat a kerosene lamp with the chimney missing and the wick turned to black. The chimney was eventually found beneath a dresser. Another lamp was found at the end of the guest bed, where the bodies of the Stillinger girls lay. It too had the chimney missing. The axe itself, although covered in blood, showed signs that the killer had tried to wipe away the blood to no avail. The axe was found to belong to Josiah. In the bedroom downstairs, a small piece of keychain was found that didn't seem to belong to anyone in the house. On the table in the kitchen was a pan containing bloody water and a plate of food that hadn't been touched. Up in the attic, two cigarette butts were located, and it was assumed that the killer (perhaps killers) had waited up there for the family to return home. This was perhaps the most terrifying piece of evidence—to think that this innocent family returned home following a pleasant evening only to be ambushed by someone waiting inside.

Who Were the Suspects?

There were numerous suspects on the list, and one was even arrested and tried for the crime, though eventually he was acquitted. They ranged from transients to a reverend, and even a serial killer, but nobody was ever held accountable and brought to justice for this horrific massacre of the Moore family and the Stillinger girls.

Andrew Sawyer

Naturally, any transients or strangers were considered suspicious during the investigation into the murders. This is generally because people as a rule don't trust strangers, and nobody wants to consider that maybe it was someone they knew. In small towns in particular, people are more wary of those they don't know. One such man that fit this bill was Andrew Sawyer.

There was never any concrete evidence to suggest Sawyer had played a part in the killings. Instead, he was brought to light by a gentleman who worked for the railroad and had interacted with Sawyer on the morning of the murders in nearby Creston. Thomas Dyer alleged that Sawyer had appeared around 6 a.m. that morning looking for work. He was dressed in a brown suit, was shaven, his pants were wet almost up to his knees, and his shoes were covered in mud. Workers were highly sought after, so he was hired there and then. Later that evening, Sawyer apparently bought a newspaper with the murders broadcast across the front page, and he went off alone to read it.

Apparently, Sawyer was very interested in the murders, and he talked about them often with his fellow workers. Even more strange, he had a habit of sleeping with his axe next to him. He would later tell Dyer that he had been in Villisca the night of the murders but had left for fear of being considered a suspect. When considering all of the strange behaviors he had exhibited, Dyer handed Sawyer over to the sheriff on June 18, 1912.

Despite the statements Sawyer had made to his work colleagues and the intense interest he seemed to show in the murders, even placing himself in town on the night in question, it would later be proven that he was innocent. On investigation, it turned out that Sawyer had been arrested on that very night in a town called Osceola, also in Iowa, for vagrancy. Therefore, he had an alibi.

The Reverend George Kelly

Kelly was a man with a disturbing background who happened to be at the very same Children's Day services the Moore family and the Stillinger sisters attended that day, June 9, 1912. Born in England, Kelly was a traveling minister who many regarded as being rather odd. It was claimed that he had suffered some type of mental breakdown when he was younger, and his adult behavior included lewd acts such as peeping and trying to get young girls to pose for him in the nude. Strangely, he left Villisca somewhere between 5 a.m. and 5:30 a.m., just hours after the murders had occurred and before the bodies were found.

Over the following weeks, he showed a strong fascination with the case. He began to write letters to the investigators, the police, and even the mourning family members. As expected, this behavior seemed suspicious to the investigators, and they in turn wrote back asking if Kelly happened to know anything about the killings. Kelly replied that he may have witnessed the crimes being committed and had heard sounds that evening. However, due to his history of mental illness, the police were unsure whether he was recalling facts because he was involved or whether he was just making it all up.

Kelly was arrested on a different matter in 1914, after having sent obscene material to a woman who had applied to work for him. As a result he was sent to a mental health hospital in Washington, which left the police unsure if he was the killer or not. However, in 1917 they decided to interrogate Kelly again, and following several hours of questioning, Kelly confessed to the crimes. Later he would recant this confession, claiming to be innocent after all. Two trials followed, and the jury obviously agreed with him, as the first trial resulted in a hung jury and the second led to an acquittal.

State Senator Frank F. Jones

As a suspect, Senator Jones was perhaps the least likely to have been behind the murders. However, there was a rumor that he had hired William 'Blackie' Mansfield to commit the crimes following an issue that had arisen between the Senator and Josiah Moore. Josiah at one time had worked for the Senator at his implement shop for several years and then left his employment so he could open up his own store. This resulted in the Senator losing a lot of his customers to Josiah, including a very lucrative dealership with John Deere. There were also rumors around town that Josiah and the Senator's daughter-in-law had an affair, though this was never substantiated. Would a man such as the State Senator have ordered the assassination of an entire family over something such as lost business and possible adultery? The investigators clearly didn't think so, as this matter was not taken any further, at least where the Senator was concerned. Mansfield, on the other hand, was an entirely different matter.

William 'Blackie' Mansfield

Mansfield came to light as a potential suspect not only because of the rumor of his being hired by the Senator, but also because of murders he subsequently committed following the massacre in the Moore household. Two years after the murders in Villisca, Mansfield was suspected of murdering his wife, child, father-in-law and mother-in-law in very similar circumstances, which made the authorities take a much closer look at Mansfield. He was linked by circumstance to the axe murders in Colorado Springs just nine months before Villisca and another axe murder in Ellsworth, Kansas. He was also suspected of being the perpetrator of axe murders in Paola, Kansas, just four days before the tragedy at Villisca. Furthermore, he was a prime suspect in the axe murders in Illinois of Jennie Miller and Jennie Peterson. More axe murders occurring around the same time period were also considered to be the work of one man. The similarities between all of these murders were spine-tingling.

Each of these murders was committed in the same manner, which would indicate they were done by the same person. All victims were attacked with an axe, and the mirrors in each home had been covered. A kerosene lamp was left burning with the chimney removed at the foot of each bed. A basin containing bloody water was found at each scene, where the murdered had obviously tried to clean himself. Gloves were worn at each crime scene, leaving no trace of fingerprints. The coincidences were just too good to be true, and although we have more access to media information these days, back then the chances of there being a copycat killer or killers roaming the streets were less likely.

In 1916, the Grand Jury agreed to embark on an investigation and Mansfield was arrested. He was transported from Kansas City to Montgomery County to face questioning. Despite all of the evidence that seemed to indicate he was the murderer, Mansfield was found to have a legitimate alibi for the night of the murders in Villisca and so was set free without being charged. He would then bring a lawsuit against the detective who had pursued him as a suspect, Detective James Wilkerson. Mansfield won his case and was awarded the staggering amount of $2,225. This was a huge amount in those days. Some speculated that the Senator played a part in getting Mansfield released, but this was never proven.

Henry Lee Moore

Henry, who was no relation to Josiah Moore and his family, had been convicted of a double axe murder months after the murders in Villisca. Henry had killed his mother and his grandmother, and there was much suspicion that Henry was actually a serial killer. The crimes were very similar, especially as the same type of weapon was used, but there was never any evidence to link him to the Moore family murders. He was always considered a suspect, however, and he was never completely ruled out.

Fourteen Witnesses Called to Coroner's Inquest

Remarkably, the coroner called the jury together and began the inquest on June 11, 1912, just two days after the murders had taken place. Nowadays it can take months or years for an inquest to take place, let alone in the same week! Anyway, the county coroner at the time was Dr. Linquist, and he and the members of the jury all visited the Moore house to view the scene and the bodies before they were removed. A temporary morgue was set up at the local fire station, and the bodies were finally moved there around 2 a.m. on the June 10.

A total of fourteen witnesses were called to testify at the inquest, and they were as follows:

- Mary Peckham—the neighbor who raised the alarm that something was wrong at the house
- Ed Selley—an employee of Josiah, Ed had arrived to take care of the animals
- Dr. J. Clark Cooper—the first doctor to enter the house following the discovery
- Jessie Moore—Ross Moore's wife, who took the call from Mary
- Dr. F.S. Williams—the doctor who examined the bodies

- Edward Landers—was staying just up the road at his mother's house and claimed he heard a noise around 11 p.m.
- Ross Moore—Josiah's brother, the first person to gain entry to the house
- Fenwick Moore—also Josiah's brother
- Marshall Hank Horton—the first officer to enter the house
- John Lee Van Gilder—Josiah's nephew
- Harry Moore—Josiah's brother
- Joseph Stillinger— the father of the murdered Stillinger girls
- Blanche Stillinger—sister of the murdered Stillinger girls
- Charles Moore—another of Josiah's brothers

Most of the witnesses were called to testify regarding what they had seen when entering the house that day. The descriptions given by some were gruesome to say the least, but their testimony was all consistent. Josiah's brothers were called largely to speak of any troubles Josiah may have had or been in, such as business problems. None could say that they were aware of any issues or of anyone who wished to cause the family such terrible harm. One brother, Charles, was asked to testify regarding whether the axe belonged to Josiah or not. Although he couldn't say it was for sure, he did state that Josiah owned one similar. It must have been a terrible burden on both the Moore and Stillinger families to have to endure the inquest so quickly after the tragedy. They barely had time to digest what had happened before being thrust into a courtroom to discuss it, and the details must have been truly shocking. Particularly for the father of the two little Stillinger girls who had simply gone to a friend's house for the night.

Deathbed and Jailhouse Confessions

On March 19, 1917, a reverend by the name of J.J. Burris, who was the pastor of the Church of Christ in Oklahoma, traveled to Red Oak because of a deathbed confession he had received. Burris was subpoenaed by the grand jury of Montgomery County to give evidence regarding this confession of the murders of the Moore family. Burris had claimed that a man whose name he could not remember had summoned him to his hotel room so that he could confess his sins before dying. This took place in July 1913, just over a year after the murders had been committed.

Burris stated that when he arrived at the man's room, he could tell straight away that he was near death, and despite his physical state, the man began to talk the minute he entered the room. The man claimed that he had committed many sins, but the worst was the murders in Villisca. He had been living in the town at the time, working in the blacksmith industry, and his sister had been married to a physician in Villisca before moving to Radersburg. He was unable to speak for long due to his deteriorating condition, and as such was incapable of giving any details. Burris estimated the man to be around twenty-five years old, and it was believed he had part ownership in a blacksmith business in Radersburg.

Because the story was unclear, Detective Wilkerson decided that it would not stand up in court, as too little information was available. The man who had made the confession was dead and unable to stand trial anyway. The story was pushed aside as irrelevant.

George Meyers Confesses in Jail

In March 1931, a prisoner in a county jail in Detroit who was awaiting sentencing for burglary made a startling confession, stating he was the one who had committed the axe murders in Villisca. Meyers had been under interrogation for around five hours by detectives at the time of his confession, following an anonymous tip that he was the man they were looking for. It was believed that Meyers' fingerprints had been found at the murder scene; however, this was unlikely as no fingerprints were found in the Moore house.

Meyers' confession stated that he had been hired to kill the family by a businessman, though he could not recall his name. The price on offer was $5,000—a huge amount. He claimed his name had been given to these people through acquaintances in the Kansas City underworld. This acquaintance escorted him to Villisca to meet with the man who wished to hire him. He was shown the house where the family lived and told to kill them all. A deposit payment of $2,000 was given, and Meyers was told he would receive the rest after the job was done. Meyers then entered the house shortly after midnight and slaughtered the two adults and four children with an axe. When meeting with the businessman afterwards he was told he would have to wait for the rest of the money. Meyers decided it was best to flee town before the sun came up for fear of being caught.

Now, if you read that carefully, you would see what the problem was with Meyers' confession. George Meyers only confessed to killing six people that night—two adults and four children. But there were eight killed in that house, not six. He flatly denied killing the Stillinger girls, only the Moore family. Although there had been a witness story that claimed three men had been overhead talking in the forest near the house the night of the murders about committing the crime, and this seems to fit with Meyers, his acquaintance, and the businessman, there is no way Meyers would have gotten the number of victims wrong. Therefore, it was decided that this confession was nonsense, and no further action was taken against him for the crime. To date, nobody has ever been charged with these murders, so the case remains unsolved.

CHAPTER 3:
The Disappearance of Stacy Peterson and Christie Marie Cales

One day she was there, the next she had vanished without a trace. The story of Stacy Peterson and her disappearance was one that would baffle investigators. How could someone simply vanish off the face of the earth? However, Stacy had the misfortune of being married to a man who was not at all what he seemed—Drew Peterson, police officer, husband, and murderer. Was he behind her disappearance?

The Troubled Life of Stacy

Stacy had lived a terrible childhood, fraught with fighting parents, alcohol abuse, violence, and neglect. Her mother seemed incapable of doing anything except drinking a case of beer each day and lying on the couch while the children were left to fend for themselves. They had already lost one child in a house fire and then lost a baby to SIDs later on. These tragedies most likely contributed to the volatile household and Stacy's mother's regular stays in both jail and mental hospitals.

Despite all of this, Stacy was able to stay on the right path, and she graduated from high school early at just sixteen years of age.

With a dream of becoming a nurse but unable to afford the education, Stacy took on a variety of odd jobs. When she was seventeen in 2001, she was working at a hotel as a desk clerk when she met the man she would later marry, police officer Drew Peterson. Drew was 47 years old and on his third marriage when they met, but that didn't stop either of them. Stacy saw in Drew the father figure she had never really had and a chance at a secure life. Drew divorced his wife in October 2003, and eight days later he married Stacy.

The first child they had together was a boy called Anthony, who was named after Stacy's father. She was right in her element in her role as wife and mother, and she was an excellent housewife. She believed she had a good marriage, probably because she was young and naïve. Drew would call her constantly when she went out, even if she was just going to the grocery store. He would not let her get a job, he did nothing to take care of the baby, and he more or less tried to control every aspect of her life.

In 2004, Drew's ex-wife Kathleen Savio was found dead, apparently having had an accident in the bathtub. Stacy was quick to defend her husband against any allegations that he had been behind the death, and she even provided an alibi for him. By then she had another child, Lacy, who was named after her sister who passed away, so young Stacy had two children to worry about and was desperate to keep the family together. She would do or say anything to protect her husband.

When Stacy was twenty-three, following the loss of her sister Tina to cancer, she started to make changes in her life. She started to take the children to Bible studies, had taken on a job as an Avon sales rep, and was generally taking better care of herself and her appearance. This all went against Drew's instructions, and he certainly wasn't pleased. But by now Stacy had started to question whether her husband had been involved in the death of his wife Kathleen. By October 2007, she had decided she wanted a divorce.

Just one week later, on October 28, Stacy had vanished.

Gone Without a Trace

On the day of October 28, 2007, Stacy was meant to go and help her sister with some painting, but she never arrived. She sent a text message that Sunday morning at 10:15 saying she wasn't ready to get up out of bed yet. There was no further contact. From then onward, nobody would ever hear from Stacy or see her again. She literally just vanished without a trace.

Drew claimed Stacy had called him that same night from an airport, saying she had met another man and was leaving.

Despite this story, her family reported her missing, as they knew she wouldn't have gone without her kids. Family and friends also knew that Stacy had been making plans to leave Drew, so there was no chance she would just up and go without carrying those plans through.

While the authorities and numerous volunteers scoured the area for any trace of Stacy, Drew seemed to be treating it with very little concern. He made flippant remarks and treated the whole situation as if it was a bit of a joke. When questioned about Stacy wanting a divorce, he claimed she asked him all the time for one, depending on her menstrual cycle. Drew Peterson was showing a side of himself that people hadn't seen before, and it was very unpleasant.

The night before her disappearance, Stacy had been hanging out with her sister, Cassandra Cales, and had said to her sister that if anything ever happened to her it was Drew that did it. Cassandra desperately pleaded with her sister to leave with her right then and there, but Stacy said she couldn't leave the children.

Morphey's Story

Thomas Morphey was the stepbrother of Drew, and he had quite the story to tell. The only difficulty was getting people to listen. Morphey stated he was involved in conversations with Drew over a period of two days, starting on October 27, wherein he was convinced Drew was planning to murder someone. It all started with Drew arriving at Morphey's residence and asking him to go for a ride to a nearby park. Allegedly, Drew asked him if he loved him enough to kill for him, to which Morphey replied no, he would be unable to live with himself. Drew then asked if he could live with himself knowing about it. To this question Morphey replied yes, further adding that they had already assumed Drew had killed Kathleen.

Drew then proceeded to tell Morphey that Stacy had been unfaithful and that he had seen her out with other men, and something had to be done about it. He then drove them to a storage facility and asked Morphey to rent a locker for him, and told him if he put it in his own name, he would be paid $2,000. Assuming Drew was planning to store a body there, Morphey was concerned that it would smell. Drew replied that it would be in a sealed container, so it wouldn't be a problem. It was at that very point Morphey knew Drew was going to murder someone, but he didn't realize it would be Stacy. He thought it would be the man she was allegedly having an affair with.

Despite Drew's persuasion, Morphey couldn't rent the locker, as he didn't have any identification with him. He returned home, and after a few hours he called Drew and told him he didn't want to be involved in anything, and Drew stated he respected his wishes. However, the following day Drew arrived at Morphey's residence completely unannounced and again asked to go for a ride to the park. When they reached the park, Morphey was given a cell phone and told not to answer it. Drew then left, leaving Morphey to wonder what was going on.

The phone rang twice, forty-five minutes after Drew had left Morphey in the park. The caller ID showed the calls were coming from Stacy's cell phone, and he suddenly realized that Drew was setting it up to murder Stacy. He assumed Drew was driving around to various locations so the cell phone would ping off different towers when police investigated. An hour later, Drew came back, picked up Morphey, and took back the cell phone. Morphey again told Drew that he didn't want to be involved and that he wanted to go home. Drew said he just needed to pop over to the house for a minute. Despite his disagreement, Morphey went along with him.

Morphey waited outside the house, and out came Drew with a large blue barrel. Drew was unable to get it down the stairs on his own, so Morphey had to help him. They then loaded it into the back of the truck. Morphey was driven home and instructed that 'none of this ever happened'. Despite not actually assisting with the murder of Stacy, the fact that he had been involved with the suspicious phone calls and had helped to carry the barrel which most likely contained her body, created so much guilt that the following day Morphey attempted suicide. His wife rushed him to the hospital, and once he had recovered, he was taken to the police by his brother. Even though he had been somewhat involved, he was granted immunity from prosecution and placed under police protection for six months while he waited to be called by the grand jury.

The lawyer acting for Drew, Joel Brodsky described Morphey's story as a tale dreamt up by an alcohol and drug addict. He did not believe Morphey was a credible witness because of his problems with addiction and therefore would be unlikely to ever be called to testify.

Kathleen Savio

While married to Vicki Connolly, Drew embarked on an affair with Kathleen Savio. His marriage to Vicki was falling apart due to his infidelities and controlling behavior, and they divorced in 1992. Soon after the divorce was finalized, Kathleen and Drew were married. They would go on to have two sons, Kristopher and Thomas. The marriage was not a happy one for very long, and in 2002 Kathleen got a protection order against her husband due to physical abuse. By 2003, Drew was involved with Stacy, and he and Kathleen divorced. However, the financial issues of the marriage were never finalized, and they were still trying to come to an agreement in April 2004. A hearing was set, but Kathleen would never attend, as by March 1, 2004, she was dead.

Kathleen's body was found in her bathtub at home. There was no water in the bathtub, and there were some injuries to her body, yet the physician who performed the initial autopsy claimed it was an accidental death. He surmised that she had slipped in the bathtub and hit her head, drowning, and that was the cause of death. Drew had seemed to get away with it, until his fourth wife Stacy disappeared and the police decided to take another look at the death. Stacy had admitted to at least three people in the days leading up to her disappearance that she believed Drew had murdered Kathleen, so this accusation was taken very seriously.

A second autopsy was conducted on Kathleen, with surprising results. The front of her body was covered in bruises, and Dr. Larry Blum believed these were fresh. There were scrape marks down her back, and he brushed away the initial autopsy report stating these were from rubbing against the back of the bathtub as ridiculous. The surface of the tub was incredibly smooth, and there was nothing there that could have made those marks. The back of Kathleen's head had a wound that had split the skin but not the skull beneath. Blum determined this was most likely from a direct blow. His final determination was that Kathleen had been subjected to a brutal attack shortly before her death and that her death was not an accident at all.

Another Wife Murdered? The Trial of Drew Peterson

Drew was indicted on two counts of first degree murder in 2009, in relation to Kathleen Savio's death. He was held in custody from May and stayed there until his trial. A lot of the evidence against Drew would normally be considered hearsay, but due to a special law passed in Illinois in 2008, exceptions could be made in some cases.

The trial began in July 2012, after much negotiation regarding the secondhand witness statements and as to what would be allowed and what would not. Of the fourteen statements handed to the judge, only eight were approved for use during the trial. The prosecution team had requested a mistrial, but Peterson himself withdrew this request, as he wanted the current jury to hear his case. The trial would last months, until the final verdict was given on September 6, 2012. Drew Peterson was found guilty and convicted of the first degree murder of Kathleen and was sentenced to sixty years in prison. But that wasn't to be the end of courtrooms for Drew.

Drew was charged of trying to organize a hit on the Will County State's Attorney James Glasgow in February 2015. This had come about following a year of Drew's activities between September 2013 and December 2014, when he had been trying to arrange for the attorney's murder. He was charged with one count of solicitation of murder and one count of solicitation of murder for hire.

Now that Drew had been found guilty of the murder of his ex-wife Kathleen, the family and friends of Stacy Peterson began to push for further investigation into her disappearance. It seemed more than likely that if he could murder one wife to be rid of a perceived problem, then surely it would be easy for him to do the same to another wife. To this day, he still claims she ran away with another man.

Disappearance of Her Mother—Christie Marie Cales

Christie's life had been one of pain, suffering and addiction. Having tragically lost two children, Christie embarked on a downward spiral that would see her consumed by an addiction and having to go into mental institutions for treatment. She seemed completely incapable of dealing with daily life, and her children to husband Anthony Cales were left to take care of themselves. The marriage continued to deteriorate, and Christie had a habit of disappearing sometimes for weeks. In 1990, Christie was arrested for stealing cigarettes from a store and was then caught driving while under the influence in alcohol. The family was in serious trouble, and financial matters had reached the point where there were two foreclosures on the family home.

That same year, Anthony filed for divorce, unable to cope with Christie's behavior and the effects on the family any longer. Initially Christie contested the divorce, but she repeatedly missed the court hearings, and Anthony was granted full and sole custody of the children. Christie moved in with other family members, and eventually Anthony and the children moved to Florida. Despite the distance, Christie was still able to see the children from time to time.

Christie met another man and moved in with him. In 1998, Christie left the house carrying her bible and purse and was never seen or heard from again. There were different witness statements, with some saying Christie had said she was going to church, which would make sense given the bible she was carrying, and others saying she was going shopping. Because Christie had a history of disappearing now and then, it wasn't taken too seriously at first. However, her daughters Stacy, Cassandra, and Tina, all believed she was murdered, and they suspected Christie's boyfriend of being the killer. They tried to make a case with the local police, but they failed to agree, and no investigation was undertaken.

It is so ironic and tragic that both mother and daughter would disappear, leaving friends and family to wonder what ever happened to them. One thing is for sure—both are most likely to have been murdered.

CHAPTER 4:
Lucia de Berk – Angel of Death?

Unlike the previous chapters where the focus was on a murder victim, in this case the victim is still very much alive. Lucia de Berk was a pediatric nurse in her home country of the Netherlands, and due to an investigation into unexplained deaths of patients in her care, she was subsequently arrested, charged, and found guilty of murder and attempted murder. However, Lucia was not the angel of death so many suspected at all. Instead, she was a victim of a terrible miscarriage of justice which almost saw her put behind bars for the rest of her natural life.

Accused of Seven Cases of Murder and Three Cases of Attempted Murder

Lucia was working as a pediatric nurse at the Juliana Children's Hospital in The Hague, Netherlands, when an investigation into suspicious deaths during hospital admissions was undertaken. On September 4, 2001, a baby died suddenly while in the hospital, and this triggered an investigation into any unexpected deaths or resuscitation attempts. It was found that there had been nine incidents between September 2000 and September 2001, which originally were thought to be natural deaths but on further inspection of the records appeared to be highly suspicious.

One nurse had been on duty on the occasion of each of these deaths—Lucia. At the time, she was responsible for giving medication and managing the care of each patient. To the hospital, it seemed too much of a coincidence that she had been taking care of each of these nine patients before they suddenly died, and they proceeded to press charges against Lucia.

The Trial and Sentencing

The allegations against Lucia involved cases from three hospitals in the immediate area, all of which had suspicious deaths occur while she was on duty and present. She was brought to trial in March 2003, and was only charged with the deaths and attempted deaths that the medical experts concluded had no natural causes. It was suggested that Lucia had poisoned each patient, resulting in cardiac arrest and death. In some cases the patients had been saved by cardiopulmonary resuscitation, but Lucia was still charged with attempted murder in these cases.

During the trial, Lucia's character was naturally brought into question. It was alleged that she had once worked as a prostitute while living in Canada and also in the Netherlands, before she became a nurse. It was also alleged that she suffered from depression, and her own brother claimed she was an avid liar and he believed she was capable of committing murder.

But what really sealed the fate of Lucia was the judiciary relying on statistical reports that showed that the probability of a nurse being on duty during each incident was 1 in 342 million. With such staggering odds, the trial only lasted five days, and at the end Lucia was found guilty of the murders and attempted murders on March 24, 2003. The sentence she received was life imprisonment, and in the Netherlands, life meant life.

The first appeal was put forward on June 18, 2004. This was rejected, and the conviction was upheld. Lucia was also sentenced to detention with psychiatric treatment, even though the criminal psychologist assigned by the state could find no evidence that she was suffering from a mental illness. The case was then presented to the Netherlands Supreme Court in March 2006, at which time it was deemed incorrect to impose a psychiatric detention at the same time as life imprisonment. Despite this, the Supreme Court returned the case back to the court in Amsterdam to reevaluate any facts that had arisen to support an appeal. Just days after the Supreme Court had made its ruling, Lucia suffered a stroke and was admitted to the prison hospital. On July 13, 2006, the Court of Appeal upheld the initial verdict and conviction, and the life sentence was given once again. This time however, the psychiatric detention was dismissed.

Doubts Emerge

Many people had begun to support Lucia, and a committee was created that continuously expressed doubts about her conviction and sentence. One of these doubts pertained to the usage of chain-link proof, wherein a person found guilty without reasonable doubt in one case is therefore guilty in subsequent cases. For Lucia, that meant that because she was found guilty of two of the murders, the court system therefore concluded she must be guilty of the others. This also means that evidence does not need to be terribly strong in all of the cases.

The two murders that were supposedly proven were based on the fact that the medical experts were unable to find the deaths were caused by natural causes. Digoxin was the drug suspected of poisoning in both of the patients, and it was supposedly detected in samples from one child by two separate laboratories. However, the methods used were not refined enough to exclude that it could have actually been a similar substance the body naturally produces. The samples were sent to another laboratory, the Strasbourg Laboratory, which used a newer method that tests for sensitivity and high specificity, meaning the analysis was more delicate. They found that there was no evidence to support the presence of digoxin, and so the allegation of death by poisoning with this drug was not conclusive.

For the other child, it was surmised that the overdose could have been due to a faulty prescription. In both cases, there were no clear signs as to how Lucia was even able to administer the digoxin. There was even evidence thrown out by the prosecution that proved Lucia wasn't in the room with one of the patients when they died. If this had been put forward during the trial, the whole synopsis of Lucia being the only one present on each occasion would have been brought into speculation and doubt.

Initially Lucia had been charged with thirteen counts of murder and medical emergencies, but the defense was able to prove that Lucia had not been present in many of these cases. At one point, she had even been away on leave, and it was simply an administrative error that put her there at the wrong time. Up until the last death that triggered the investigation, every other death later considered to be murder had been classified as being due to natural causes. Even the last case was initially put down as a natural death until it was suggested that one nurse, Lucia, had been with each patient that had died.

During the trial, the court favored the use of statistical calculations to determine the likelihood that one particular nurse may be present during so many deaths. The calculation that the chances were as low as 1 in 342 million more or less sealed Lucia's fate, as that was the statistic the court used to determine her guilt. It was later determined that the figure was closer to 1 in 25 that a nurse would be present during a spate of hospital deaths. When you consider a nurse's shifts, how often they are at the hospital, the type of wards they work in, and the size of the hospital itself, it is more than possible for one nurse to be with a number of patients as they die.

Reopening of the Case

Cases are generally not reopened in the Dutch legal system unless a new fact is presented. They don't consider different interpretations of old facts by experts. However, Tom Derksen and Metta de Noo submitted their research to the Posthumous II Commission, which looks at certain closed cases and checks for errors by the police and any misunderstanding of scientific and medical evidence. Derksen declared the medical experts had not been given all of the relevant information when questioned about the possibility of natural causes leading to the deaths. He also showed that the Strasbourg Laboratory had found there was no indication of digoxin poisoning, and that initial results were due to poor methods and techniques. The Commission agreed to look at the case and assigned three men from their group to investigate whether there had been other unexplained deaths when Lucia wasn't present, if all relevant information was given to the expert witnesses, and if scientific knowledge now altered the question regarding digoxin.

The Commission released their report in October 2007, recommending that the case be reopened due to the apparent tunnel vision of the investigators in the beginning. Also, with the last alleged victim, natural causes could no longer be ruled out, and in April 2008 Lucia was released from prison for three months. She would remain free from prison throughout the investigation and appeal process.

After months of investigation and hearings, the appeal hearing finally came to an end on March 17, 2010. It had been determined that none of the deaths were caused by deliberate action and that they were either due to natural causes, wrong treatments, poor diagnosing, or inadequate hospital management. The public prosecution made a formal request to the court to change the verdict to not guilty. The court agreed and delivered the verdict on April 14, 2010.

Justice Miscarried

Though there have been many cases of innocent people found guilty and imprisoned or even put to death in some countries, the case of Lucia de Berk was perhaps one of the worst, because there was never any evidence that a crime had even been committed. It was all based on supposition, coincidence, and failure to understand science. Lucia spent more than six years in jail, suffered a stroke, and had everything about her personal and professional life brought into question, not only in court but also in the media.

It is true that Lucia received financial compensation for the wrongful conviction and imprisonment, but the figure has never been made public. However, for someone who effectively lost six years of their life, money is probably little reward. The whole judicial process took a tremendous toll physically and mentally on a woman who was doing the job she loved, taking care of others. To be accused and convicted of such a terrible thing, and to be labelled an 'angel of death' must have been absolutely soul destroying. Yet, she continued to fight for her innocence, along with a barrage of supporters. Aside from the effect on Lucia, the families of the alleged victims must also have felt this miscarriage of justice, for they were led to believe their loved ones had been murdered for nine years. They too, like Lucia, were victims of the judicial system.

CHAPTER 5:
The Richardson Murders in Canada

The story behind the tragic murders of a family in Medicine Hat, Alberta, Canada, contains all the makings of a blockbuster movie—young love, a troubled teen, disapproving parents, alcohol and drugs, vampires and werewolves. Yes, vampires and werewolves. It will make you look twice at a person who is Goth, for all the wrong reasons. And it was a crime that would make history in Canada, as the instigator and perpetrator was none other than a 12-year-old girl and her much older boyfriend.

The Discovery of the Crime Scene

The discovery of the triple homicide of the Richardson family was made initially by a young six-year-old boy who had come over to play with the youngest member of the family, Jacob, aged 8. The little boy peered through a window to see if anyone was home, but what he saw would undoubtedly leave him with nightmares for many years to come. Lying on the floor of the basement, in clear view, were the bloodied bodies of two adults who weren't moving. The alarm was raised, and authorities rushed to the scene.

On entering the house, they found Marc Richardson, 42, and his wife Debra, 48, dead on the floor. It was obvious they had suffered numerous stab wounds, and authorities continued their search through the house to see if there were any further victims. Upstairs, the small body of Jacob was found with his throat cut. Those who knew the family immediately became concerned about the whereabouts and safety of the fourth member of the Richardson family, their daughter Jasmine.

The body of Marc contained more than twenty-four stab wounds, including nine in his back. His wife Debra had been stabbed at least twelve times, and their young son had a gaping wound in his throat. Bloody handprints and smears were found throughout the basement on the walls, and there was still no sign of Jasmine. The search was now on for Jasmine, for fear she had been abducted or murdered elsewhere.

A Shocking Suspect

The day after the discovery of the murdered Richardson family members, Jasmine was finally located in Leader, Saskatchewan, around 81 miles away from Medicine Hat. With her was her boyfriend, Jeremy Allan Steinke, 23, and his friend Kacy Lancaster, 19. Immediately, all three were arrested by the police and returned to Medicine Hat. During the search for evidence at the crime scene, the police had discovered several online accounts with which Jasmine and Jeremy had been talking to each other about murdering her parents, so they knew immediately who the suspects were. Kacy Lancaster was arrested and charged with being an accessory because she had driven them in her truck away from the location and had helped with disposing of evidence.

Both Jasmine and Jeremy were charged with three counts of murder, and at the tender age of twelve, Jasmine became the youngest person to ever be charged with multiple murders in Canada. Because of her age, the Youth Criminal Justice Act prevented her name from being published once she was deemed a suspect. Also under Canadian law, any suspect who is under fourteen years of age cannot be tried as an adult, and the maximum sentence that can be given is ten years. The same luck didn't apply to Jeremy, as at the age of twenty-three he was most certainly an adult and would be tried as such.

Jasmine's trial began in June 2007, and by then she had turned fourteen. The charges were three counts of first degree murder, to which she plead not guilty to all. Her trial lasted about a month, and in July she was found guilty of all counts by the jury, who had needed just three hours of deliberation. Sentencing for Jasmine took place in November of the same year, and, as expected, she was sentenced to ten years in prison. Part of her sentence required her to spend four years in a psychiatric hospital, and after the term of her full sentence, she would be placed under conditional supervision within the community for a further four and a half years. Her sentence was due to be completed in 2015, by which time she would have turned twenty-three years old.

Steinke Goes on Trial

By all accounts, Jeremy Steinke was a disturbed young man. Some men will do anything for love, and Jeremy really took this to the extreme by helping his very young girlfriend murder her family. Of course, it's not the first time this has happened, and no doubt it will happen again. At the age of twenty-three, Jeremy had not matured very much at all and had made claims that he was a vampire, a werewolf, and a Gothic. With piercings, tattoos, a love of blood, kink fetishes, and razorblades, it's no wonder alarm bells were ringing with Jasmine's parents. Unfortunately, those same alarm bells were not being heard by the authorities.

The night of the murders, Jeremy stated he had been drinking red wine and beer and had consumed a considerable amount of cocaine. He then climbed through an open window into the basement of the Richardson home and waited. Debra heard a noise downstairs and went down to check it out, and she must have been shocked to see Jeremy standing there armed with a knife. He grabbed her and started stabbing her over and over again.

Marc Richardson was the next to die. He too heard a noise and went down to the basement. While being attacked by Jeremy, Marc fought back as hard as he could, armed with nothing more than a screwdriver, but it was no use. Allegedly, as he was dying Marc asked Jeremy why he was doing this, and Jeremy explained it was what Jasmine wanted. Imagine that being the last thing a father hears. There was no doubt that Jeremy had killed the parents, but the murder of their eight-year-old son Jacob was not as clear.

While in custody, Jeremy had mistakenly had a conversation with someone he thought was another inmate but in fact was an undercover cop. Jeremy was open about the crime, claiming responsibility to the undercover cop, and it was this conversation that turned the opinion around regarding the death of young Jacob. According to Jeremy, it was Jasmine that had slit her little brother's throat and watched him die. To make it even more chilling, she allegedly showed no emotion, guilt, or remorse while doing so.

Jeremy had a pretty big mouth and made numerous statements to a variety of people about his role in the crime. He had told friends that he had "gutted her parents like fish." Right after the murders, they even went to a friend's house and had sex. And it was another friend that helped them get away from the town that night. Whether these people were afraid of Jeremy for some reason, or maybe just didn't care about what he and Jasmine had done, is disturbing.

On November 17, 2008, Jeremy's trial began in Calgary. The trial was originally going to take place in Medicine Hat, but Jeremy's legal team asked for the move so that the jury wouldn't be swayed by public knowledge at the time. It really wouldn't have made much difference, as the story of the murders had become a national news event, and the outcome would most likely have been the same regardless of where the trial took place.

Testimony included numerous statements from friends and associates, some of whom had been asked to help with the murders and declined. There were also internet and computer conversations where the two of them had openly discussed their plan to kill Jasmine's parents, including different methods of killing. Kacy Lancaster, who drove them to Saskatchewan the night of the murders, claimed she knew nothing about what they had just done. She stated she only found out after reading the newspaper, and she noted that both Jeremy and Jasmine showed no emotion about it at all. She had also noticed there was blood in Jeremy's truck, along with weapons including baseball bats and knives.

Not surprisingly, Jeremy was found guilty of first degree murder for each of the victims. On December 15, 2008, he was handed down three life sentences. They are concurrent sentences, and Jeremy will be eligible for parole after twenty-five years, in 2031.

A Lethal Romance

There were so many things wrong with this romance, it's hard to know where to begin. Jasmine and Jeremy had apparently met in the early part of 2006, with some saying the meeting happened at a punk rock concert, while others say it started as an online romance. In any case, Jeremy was twenty-three years old at the time, and Jasmine was just twelve. You have to wonder what a man of that age would see in such a young girl, but they quickly became a couple.

Naturally, Jasmine's parents were totally against the relationship and had every right to be. Not only was the age difference a huge problem, but it was Jeremy's background and character that worried them the most. At one point Jeremy claimed to be a 300-year-old werewolf. An adult would see through this as nonsense, but a 12-year-old child may not have the maturity to see through it. If you put yourself in Jasmine's shoes, she had a much older man interested in her, a man that seemed (to her) to be worldly and be interested in the same dark interests as herself. He told her he loved her, and he most probably did, and for a young girl, that's all she would need to hear. Don't be mistaken in thinking she was the victim, however—this girl, despite her age, knew how to manipulate her boyfriend extremely well.

Girls often go for the 'bad boy', and in the case of Jasmine and Jeremy, they thought of themselves as soulmates, lovers that would be together for ever. The only thing standing in their way (despite the obvious statutory rape law) was her parents. They were completely opposed to the relationship, and had instructed Jasmine not to see Jeremy anymore. A young teenage girl, Jasmine was adamant that she wanted to spend the rest of her life with Jeremy, and so it was her that came up with the idea of killing her parents. In her mind, that was the only way they could be together. Jeremy, being the love-sick dutiful boyfriend, agreed, and so the stage was set for what would be one of the most disturbing multiple murders ever committed in Medicine Hat.

Once both had been arrested and held in custody, they continued to communicate with each other for a long time. Their letters contained dreams and plans that one day they would run away together and get married. However, the relationship broke down and crumbled when Jeremy stated during his trial that he did not kill young Jacob and that it had been Jasmine who dealt the fatal wound. Jasmine had categorically stated that she had no part in the actual killings. She would have seen Jeremy's statement as a betrayal, and so she stopped communicating with him.

The Aftermath

Jeremy would attempt to launch an appeal, but not in 2012. He claimed it took him so long because he didn't know the system and the processes, and his defense attorney no longer wished to represent him. Normally following a murder conviction, if an appeal is to be lodged it is done so almost immediately. However, Jeremy subsequently withdrew his appeal and continues to sit in prison.

Things were very different for Jasmine. Her sentence as a minor was nothing at all like the hard time Jeremy is doing, and yet she seemed to be the main instigator of the crime. With only a ten-year sentence applicable due to her age, she completed her mandatory four years in a psychiatric facility and a further four and a half years in the community under supervision. Now twenty-two years of age, Jasmine is attending college and living with only minimum conditions as imposed by the courts. It is almost as though she got away with everything, even though it was her idea. If she had been a little bit older when the crimes were committed, things would have been very different for her.

CHAPTER 6:
The Good Hart Murders

The upper-middle-class Robison family from Detroit was vacationing at their cabin in Lake Michigan, north of Good Hart, when they met a horrific fate. It was 1968, and the family had decided to spend their whole summer at the cabin, a secluded spot surrounded by dense woods and tall trees. It was almost impossible to see the cabin from the road, which would lead investigators to believe the crime was committed by someone who knew the family and knew they would be there.

Family on Vacation

The Robison family consisted of Richard, 42, his wife Shirley, and their four children, Richie, 19, Gary, 17, Randy, 12, and Susan, aged 7. Richard owned and operated a small advertising agency called R.C. Robison & Associates and also published a magazine called Impresario. His wife of twenty years, Shirley, took good care of the home and the family, and they all attended church regularly. The children were all thought of as good students and well-mannered young people, with the eldest son Richie attending university at the time of the murders.

The family decided to go on vacation from their home in Lathrup Village, Michigan, to their cabin they had named Summerset, which was nestled on the banks of Lake Michigan near Good Hart. The family was considered to be well off, with Richard owning his company, as well as owning and piloting his own plane, and the adults attending theater regularly. They were good, honest folk who didn't gamble, drink, smoke, or get involved in any other activities deemed risky or of poor social status.

On July 22, 1968, a nearby neighbor had called the caretaker of the area, Monnie Bliss, claiming she was trying to hold a bridge game in her home, and there was an awful smell coming from the Robison's cabin. Many people were aware that the Robison's were meant to be going away at some time, so the caretaker wondered if an animal had crawled into the home and died, so he went to investigate. He knocked on the door but received no answer. Bliss opened the door, and the sight that greeted him made him alert the authorities immediately.

A Horrific Crime Scene

The local deputies converged on the scene and braced themselves for what they had been told was inside the cabin. On entering, they encountered masses of dead flies on the floor and pools of blood that had congealed. The bodies were noticed immediately, and all seemed to be dressed as though they were going out somewhere on their last day alive. There was even a suitcase partially packed sitting on one of the beds. It was estimated that the family had been dead for about four weeks, given the extent of the decomposition, and the local hospital refused to take them due to their state. Ludicrously, a chicken coop at a nearby fairground was used as a temporary morgue where the autopsies could be completed.

There was a difference with how Shirley Robison was left after she had been murdered. Her skirt had been pushed up and her underwear was down around her ankles. It was not certain if she had been raped, as the medical examiner failed to find any evidence as such, but the way her body was posed does indicate some sort of sexual assault had occurred. At the time of the murder, Shirley had been wearing a sanitary napkin, and it had seven perforations in it, almost like stab wounds. This could also indicate a sexual attack had occurred.

All of the victims had been shot, and both Richard and young Susan had also been bludgeoned with a hammer. Why that was necessary is not known. Shooting a child is one thing, but to strike her with a hammer is macabre. The date of death was eventually put down as Tuesday afternoon or evening on June 25, 1968. During the crime scene investigation, gas masks had to be worn to deal with the horrific odor from the decaying bodies.

The Emmet County prosecutor at the time, Wayne Richard Smith, commented that the suit he wore that day was never worn again. He ended up burning it.

Evidence and Theories

From what the crime scene showed, the killer had approached the house around twilight and initially fired shots into the living room using a .22 caliber rifle. Richard had been sitting in an easy chair and was struck in the chest. The other family members would have been stunned, so it was easy for the killer to shoot them as he burst in through the front door. Randy, Shirley, and Susan were shot as he entered, and as Richie and Gary raced from the room to the back bedroom to retrieve a gun from the closet, they too were shot and killed. For some unknown reason, the killer then went back to Susan and struck her in the head with a hammer. To ensure they were all finished off, each member of the Robison family was then shot one more time in the head.

With the amount of gunfire that took place inside the cabin, it's a wonder nobody raised the alarm. But those that lived the closest were out at the time, and those who did hear gunshots and shouting assumed that because it was still quite light outside perhaps the Robison's were out by the beach shooting gulls.

As the murderer was leaving the house, he dragged Richard, Randy, and Susan into the hallway and put a blanket over Shirley. The killer then closed all of the curtains and turned up the heat before locking the door on his way out. The last thing he did at the scene was to cover a broken window with cardboard and tape a note to it that said 'will be back—Robison'. Presumably, this was to make anyone think the family was simply away for a day or two, giving the killer enough time to make his escape without being noticed in the vicinity.

There were many theories tossed about during the investigation into these murders. Some of the local residents were concerned there was a random madman on the loose, and they feared for their own safety. At the time there was a serial killer by the name of John Norman Collins, aka the 'co-ed killer,' operating in the area, but his modus operandi was far different, so it was not likely to be him. Nevertheless, he came under suspicion simply because he was a murderer acting locally.

The Suspects

Richard Robison

The first direction the police looked was towards Richard and his business and personal life. Often when a family is assassinated in such a way, it is the act of someone close to one of the victims. On looking into Richard's life, investigators found that he wasn't really the man everyone thought he was. They uncovered the secret that he had several affairs during his marriage to Shirley. Could this then be the work of a jealous lover or an irate husband? He also liked to bring his secretary into his office and ask her to lift her skirt so he could look at her legs. Although there was no intercourse with the secretaries, he would touch and fondle them for up to an hour at a time.

The wonderful businessman, deemed a pillar of society, had also done some very suspicious business dealings, resulting in some clients being swindled by up to $50,000. Over a three year period, he would bill the client for advertisements he either didn't pay for or didn't even run. Richard would also create and publish full-page ads for airlines without asking for their permission so that his magazine would look as though it was more successful than it actually was.

Richard had come up with a scheme to create giant computerized warehouses at airports internationally. He was looking to raise $100 million from a group of investors referred to as the 'Superior Table'. He claimed this group was a global organization dedicated to bringing peace and unity among all countries. The chairman of the group was allegedly a man named Roebert. Robison even wore a St. Christopher medal with an inscription from Roebert which read: 'Richard—to my chosen son and heir —God bless you—Roebert.' Before the

Robison family left for their ill-fated vacation, Richard had been dropping hints around that he was expecting a visit from a 'Mr. Roberts' while they would be at the cabin to talk about a multi-million dollar deal. However, nobody by that name ever flew in through the nearest airport, and detectives wondered if Mr. Roberts and Roebert were the same man, or if they even ever existed.

Organized Crime

There was a large possibility that there was an organized crime link to the murders for a variety of reasons. First, one of Richard's former secretaries went on to marry a powerful and very rich manufacturing tycoon who was rumored to have ties with organized crime in Cleveland. Around the same time as the murders, the secretary had suffered a miscarriage, and there were that the baby was Robison's and not her husbands after all.

As mentioned before, Richard had swindled a number of families out of substantial amounts of money. One of those families was allegedly associated with organized crime, so the detectives had to consider the murders were a hit as payback. Also, one of the weapons used in the murders, the AR-7, was very popular among the Mafia hit men at that time. Another rumor was that Robison was behind in his payments to the mob, and if he had paid when he was supposed to, they would still be alive.

Bloxom, Brock, and Matthews

Early in 1970, an inmate at Leavenworth prison in Kansas told a story to the detectives that implicated himself and two other men in the murders of the Robison's. The inmate was Alexander Bloxom, referred to as a career criminal, who had been living in a halfway house with a man named Mark Warren Brock back in 1968. He had driven Brock to a restaurant in Flint for a meeting with a man he thought was called 'Scollata'. Afterwards, Brock traveled to Toledo and collected some weapons. He then headed north with another man named Robert Matthews. Bloxom had stayed behind because he was told there weren't any colored people in Good Hart. Two days after the murders, Brock returned.

Bloxom had the ability to recall a lot of detail. He perfectly described Richard Robison's briefcase, which he claimed Brock returned home with and destroyed later. He also had in his possession a black suitcase with guns inside, among other items, including a photograph of the Robison's and cancelled checks. These items were to be kept for future blackmail purposes, and Bloxom was instructed to get rid of the suitcase at a salvage yard in Alabama. The envelope was hidden at a relative's home.

According to Bloxom, Brock had told him they went to the cabin and knocked on the door, and he then faked having a heart attack. He lay down on the floor, and as Richard tried to help him, Matthews came in to the cabin and opened fire. He also said the wife was shot first, then one of the children who had tried to run, and then they just killed them all.

Brock was in prison when Bloxom's story came out, and he actually verified almost every detail of the story. He even admitted he wouldn't be opposed to carrying out a murder for the right price, but he was adamant he did not murder the Robison family. The three men—Bloxom, Brock and Matthews—were given polygraph tests to confirm or rule out their story. Surprisingly, Matthews passed his test. Bloxom was eager to do his test, but he ended up failing it. Brock flat out refused to take a polygraph test. Without definite corroboration or evidence, the theory that Brock and Matthews had killed the Robison's was inconclusive, so none of the men were charged.

Monnie Bliss the Caretaker

Many of the locals in the area pointed the finger at Monnie Bliss as being the culprit. His father and he had actually built the homes in the area, including the Robison cabin, and it was afterwards that Bliss took up residency as the main caretaker. Who better to do repairs on the cabins than the very man himself who built them? Despite his handyman skills, Bliss was known to have a short temper and would often be found talking to himself. Some of the locals were even afraid of Bliss, thinking he was a bit odd.

So why would Bliss murder the Robison's? It turns out, when his 18-year-old son was killed in a motorcycle accident while riding drunk, Bliss held the Robison family accountable. Apparently, his son had been with the older Robison boys that same day. To make matters worse, the day before the funeral, Richard had visited the family to offer his condolences and explain they would be unable to attend the funeral. That might not have been so bad, except that Richard then gave his wife just $20 towards flowers, which Bliss found insulting. It was the very next night the family was murdered.

Some investigators felt that the female victims were subject to overkill and were therefore the target of revenge. The use of a hammer on Susan also brought suspicion on Bliss, as he was a builder by trade, so naturally would own a hammer. There was even a rumor that his hammer had gone missing from his toolbox. However, the police considered this information to be the result of locals having a chat over a beer and speculating, rather than fact, and Bliss was cleared as a suspect. His behavior continued to be more and more bizarre, and at times he was heard to say he thought the Robison's had it coming. In some cases, he claimed he had killed the family during his semi-crazy ramblings.

The Co-Ed Killer

The co-ed killer was otherwise known as John Norman Collins, a man who was charged with one murder but suspected of up to fifteen more. He operated in California and Michigan between 1967 and 1969, and his victims were young women. His murderous spree came to an end when his uncle, a state police corporal, became suspicious. Collins had actually used his uncle's house to murder an 18-year-old woman named Karen Sue Beineman, a student at the same university Collins attended. Ironically, another fellow student at the East Michigan University was none other than Richie Robison.

Stories came about that Richie and Collins were in the same fraternity there and would therefore have known each other. Others claimed that the two had met during orientation at the university, and Collins could have visited Richie at the family cottage in Good Hart where the murders eventually took place. This would show that Collins knew where the secluded cabin was, an important factor in investigating the crime. Police never considered Collins a strong suspect, but they kept him in the back of their minds as a potential lead.

Collins adamantly denies taking any part in the murders of the Robison family. He is serving a life sentence for the murder of Karen Beineman and has stated that being convicted of one murder is one thing, but to be labelled for things he hadn't done was unfair. It's important to remember, the other murders he was suspected of committing have never been proven to be the work of Collins.

Joseph R. Scolaro – Embezzler?

Within two weeks of the investigation following the discovery of the Robison bodies, the police had a very firm suspect in mind. Joseph Scolaro was an employee of Richard's, and he had disappeared for more than twelve hours on the day of the murders. He had provided alibis for that time period, though none of them were valid. He had also recently purchased guns, the same as the ones used to commit the murders, as determined by forensic ballistic experts. These included a .25-caliber Jet-Fire automatic Beretta pistol and a .22-caliber AR-7 ArmaLite semi-automatic rifle. Forensics compared the four .22-caliber shells found at the cabin with those that had been fired by Scolaro at his family firing range, and they were found to be a match. In his defense, Scolaro claimed he had given the rifle away to someone, but a neighbor stated to police he had seen the gun at Scolaro's house not long before the murders.

Scolaro also claimed to have given away the .25-caliber pistol, and when questioned he provided a second pistol of the same caliber to the police that he had purchased at the same time as the other ones. At the crime scene were found some SAKO .25-caliber cartridges, which are a rare brand of ammunition produced in Finland. This particular ammunition is only sold during a short and specific time period each year, and one of the purchasers listed in Michigan was Scolaro. Police were able to determine that Scolaro's claims of giving away the guns were untrue, and Scolaro was unable to prove otherwise.

During their investigation, a forensic accountant was brought in to analyze the financial affairs of the Robison's and the advertising company and the magazine Richard owned. It was found that over $60,000 seemed to be missing from the company accounts. Scolaro had been left in charge of both companies for the summer while the Robison's were on vacation, and this implicated Scolaro as the killer due to embezzlement and his trying to hide his financial crime.

Despite all of this, the prosecutor was unwilling to bring charges against Scolaro without more evidence. The fact that there were no fingerprints at the crime scene and that the guns had gone missing made it difficult to prove Scolaro was ever there. Further doubts arose about the amount of time it would take Scolaro to travel from Detroit to Good Hart, kill the Robison's, and return back to Detroit. The trip one way takes between five and six hours to complete as it is, and with witnesses claim they heard gunshots around 9pm, it would be hard to comprehend how Scolaro got there and back within the twelve hours he was apparently missing. Scolaro's wife stated he was home with her by 11 p.m. that night, so if they were killed at 9 p.m., there was no possible way he could be home with his wife by then.

Furthermore, although Scolaro may have been embezzling money from his employer, it is a big jump to then turn around and murder an entire family, especially considering the brutality shown to the female victims. White-collar criminals tend to stay just that—financial fraud is quite different than physical and violent crime. Besides, although $60,000 might seem a lot to many people, it's not really the kind of figure you go on a murderous rampage for, even if you are terrified of getting caught. Unless of course the embezzlement amount was much larger. On the morning of the murders, Richard called the bank to check if a deposit he was expecting had been made, to the value of $200,000. It hadn't, so Richard immediately tried to contact Scolaro, who also had access to the account. Richard made multiple attempts to get hold of Scolaro throughout the day without any success. Back in the office, Scolaro had been told Richard was trying to get hold of him, and instead of calling him back, he just left and disappeared for the rest of the day.

Another theory was that Scolaro paid someone else to do the hit for him, which would fit in with Bloxom's story (remember the name he recalled—Scollata—is very similar). Perhaps Scolaro provided the guns, the ammunition, directions to the cabin, and could have even paid for the hit using some of the money he stole. The investigators thought there was enough evidence and information to press charges. In 1973, the prosecutor's office was on the right path to being able to file murder conspiracy charges, and Scolaro got wind of it. Shortly after, Scolaro was found dead in his office chair from a self-inflicted gunshot wound. He left a note for his mother in which he that although he was a liar, a phony and a cheat, he did not have anything to do with the murders. To others, despite what the note said, his suicide was an indication of guilt, but we'll really never know.

Nothing Resolved....Yet

To date, there has been no resolution in this multiple murder case. In 2013, detectives were still keeping an eye on the open case, and they have continued to investigate as the years have passed on. Although there have been many theories and multiple suspects, they have never been able to just narrow it down to one. With so many people now passed on, a lot of information will have died with them, so it becomes even more complicated as time passes. However, they are not giving up. They are praying for some kind of miracle, that someone will confess or at least come forward with specific information, so they can finally serve justice on the killer or killers of the Robison family.

CHAPTER 7:
Beslanowitch – The Murder of a Teen Prostitute

The killing of prostitutes is nothing new. They have been a particularly popular victim among serial killers due to their transient and high-risk lifestyle. Many of the women working the streets have few friends and very little family contact, and they can be missing for days or even weeks and months before anyone realizes they are missing. This delay is a real asset for a killer, as the more time passes, the less likely the chance is that he will be identified. It's saddening to think that these women are preyed upon simply because their lives have taken a turn for the worse. Drug addiction, abuse, alcoholism, and homelessness are all factors associated with many women who end up as prostitutes. Just because they are desperate, and even though their families may not be in touch as much, they are still human beings—someone's daughter, sister, mother, girlfriend or grandchild. They are still loved.

The Life of Krystal Beslanowitch

The body found on the banks of the Provo River near Midway, Utah, on December 15, 1995, was identified as Krystal Beslanowitch. She had grown up in Spokane, and had fallen by the wayside at the young age of fifteen years. By then, she was already involved in drugs and prostitution. Her mother has said that every time Krystal came back home, she always accepted her back. It seemed that Krystal just wasn't interested in living a normal life, despite the love and support she got at home.

Her stepfather claimed that Krystal had started selling her body much younger, at the age of twelve years old, and he also claimed she had given birth to a baby that was subsequently taken from her. He felt sorry for Krystal and believed she never really stood a chance in life. In July 1995, Krystal and her boyfriend decided to move away, and they moved to Utah. Krystal had been in trouble with the law on numerous occasions while in Spokane. The charges included prostitution, assault, drug violations, and auto theft. Perhaps they thought it was time to try their luck in a different city.

One night Krystal headed out to go to a convenience store and she never came back. Her boyfriend waited two days before he reported her missing. It's not known why he waited so long. Perhaps she had done it before and always returned. What made him more concerned was that another prostitute who had worked the same area as Krystal, west North Temple, had been murdered that November, just a month earlier.

Cold on the River Bank

Krystal went missing on a Friday, and her body was found the next day by two ranchers. They had been traveling down a country road that was quite isolated and noticed the body on the banks of the river. They notified the authorities immediately, and local law enforcement headed to the crime scene.

Krystal's body was completely nude, and it was obvious to those who saw her that she had suffered numerous traumatic blows to the head and face. The medical examiner would later confirm she had been struck at least eight or nine times with a large rock. She was just seventeen years old at the time of her death, which made it even more intolerable for the hard-nosed detectives. In fact, a sheriff's deputy named Todd Bonner was haunted by the case throughout his entire career. Once they had identified Krystal, they next had to try to find a suspect.

It wasn't going to be an easy task, and there seemed to be no leads whatsoever. It was difficult to say whether she had been murdered by a client while she was working as a prostitute or whether she was the victim of circumstance and just happened to cross paths with the wrong person at the wrong time. One thing is for sure; her boyfriend was ruled out very early on in the investigation.

During the autopsy, forensic evidence was obtained from underneath her fingernails, and forensic experts also collected evidence from the alleged murder weapon, the large rocks that had been used to bash in her head. However, forensic science wasn't as advanced back then, and it lead nowhere.

Reopening of the Case

In 2008, two detectives were assigned to reopen the case with the hopes of a breakthrough using new forensic technology. The detectives worked full time on the case, and forensic scientists were able to extract more DNA from the rocks found with her body. The DNA was run through the CODIS database and the detectives waited for a match.

The main focus of reopening the case was to further explore the forensic evidence found at the scene of the crime. Rather than re-interviewing people or revisiting the scene, attention was turned to science, and the numerous advances that had occurred. Now it was possible to get a DNA profile from a much smaller sample, and it was this that lead the police straight to the murderer.

DNA Points the Finger

All their wishes came through in January 2009, when CODIS returned a DNA match. The suspect's name was Joseph Michael Simpson, a 46-year-old man who had already served time in prison for murder back in the 1980s. He had lived in Clearfield for a time, and in 2009 was residing in Sarasota County, Florida.

The match encouraged the team to further analyze other forensic evidence from the crime scene, and this came back even stronger as belonging to Simpson. By now Todd Bonner was the Wasatch Country Sherriff, and although he wasn't heavily involved in the case, he kept his hand in it, so he was aware of what was going on at all times. Despite having the DNA match, it was decided that they needed more biological evidence from Simpson. Bonner and another detective set off to find Simpson.

They needed a fresh sample of Simpson's DNA, so they tracked him down and followed him. On August 25, 2013, they managed to follow him into a store, a smoke shop, and when he finished smoking his cigarette, Bonner grabbed it. Now they had the DNA they needed. As expected, it was a match. Simpson was subsequently arrested at his home for the murder of Krystal, and it was Bonner who had the joy of placing him in handcuffs.

He was taken to the local jail in Sarasota to await extradition back to Utah, where he would be formally charged with the murder of Krystal. Surprisingly, Simpson didn't try to fight the extradition order and was eventually returned to Utah.

Simpson's History – It Wasn't His First Murder

At the time he was arrested by Bonner, Simpson had been living in Sarasota County for nearly fourteen years. He was unemployed and living with his parents at the age of forty-six. Before then, he had lived in Clearfield, Utah. Once in custody, more information came about regarding the background of Simpson, and it was found that he had a strong history of violence.

Back in 1987, Simpson had been arrested for stabbing a man in Clearfield. It wasn't a simple stabbing —there were thirteen knife wounds in the victim, causing his death. His trial was relatively swift, and he was found guilty of second degree murder. He would go on to serve roughly eight years for the crime and was paroled in April 1995. He had only been out of prison for a few months when he murdered his next victim, Krystal.

He seemed to favor killing methods that involved being up close and personal. First was the stabbing of his first victim, as you need to be very close to a person to stab them, especially that number of times. Then, when crushing Krystal's skull with a large rock, he needed to be positioned close to or standing over Krystal to repeatedly smash the rock against her head. This method is also perhaps the most gruesome, and shows what Simpson was really capable of.

Even while in jail awaiting trial, he gained another charge of assault against a fellow inmate. As of now, he has not been sent to trial, so it is all just a matter of waiting. Despite the gravity of the crime, the prosecution has stated that they do not intend to seek the death penalty but will go for life imprisonment. Some say this is not enough. He has killed two people now, both in an extremely violent manner, and convicted criminals have been sent to death for less horrific murders. Time will tell what the outcome will be when the trial goes ahead.

CHAPTER 8:
Murder or Accident?

The case of two teenage girls disappearing into the night in 1971 had plagued the families, friends and the community for decades. They were good girls who headed out for some fun and never came back. Were they murdered? Had they been abducted? Some even wondered if they had simply run away. Or was there another reason they vanished…it would be a mystery for forty-three years.

Sherri Miller and Pam Jackson Disappear

Sherri and Pam were both from Vermilion, and both were just seventeen years old and were still attending high school. Sherri was a smart girl and was living with her grandparents after her mother had remarried then moved away. She was very independent and knew what she wanted in life and what she didn't want, a good head on her shoulders. Her grandmother had been diagnosed with terminal cancer, and Sherri willingly looked after her through the spring in 1971, as well as taking care of her grandfather. It was her job to get her grandfather out of bed in the morning, fix his breakfast, and take care of the daily chores. Because of her caring nature, she ended up working after school hours at the local Dakota Hospital, which is where her friend Pam Jackson worked as well.

Sherri wanted to go into the fashion design industry and was an avid sewer. Her plan was to move to California once she had graduated from high school, along with her cousin Pam Stewart. Pam Jackson also had an interest in dress design, and the two of them had many other things in common. On the night of May 29, 1971, Sherri had invited Pam Jackson to go out with her that night, and although Pam's mother said no at first, she ended up giving in. Pam Stewart was also going to go along with the girls, but she was called out to babysit at the last minute.

The girls made a stop at the hospital to visit with Sherri's grandmother and left there around 9:30 that night. They were driving around in Sherri's grandfather's 1960 Studebaker, a solid car that ran well. They met up with some boys from school after leaving the hospital and were invited along to a party taking place at a nearby gravel pit. The girls agreed to follow the boys there.

At one point, the boys in the car ahead had made a wrong turn, and when they doubled back there was no sign of the girls and the Studebaker. At 4 a.m. the next morning, Pam Jackson's mother noticed Pam hadn't turned off the kitchen light like she normally would when she got home. She had a look in her room and discovered she wasn't home. She assumed the girls had experienced car trouble and probably stayed in town for the night with a friend.

Later that morning, Pam's parents started to call everyone they could think of to see if the girls had spent the night, but nobody had seen them. Sherri's grandmother was critical, and in fact, she died just six days after Sherri went missing. The police naturally assumed the girls had run away, but they hadn't taken any clothing, makeup (they were teenage girls after all), or even the paychecks they had received that day. There was also no way Sherri would have abandoned her grandmother when she was so gravely ill.

The suggestion was made to drag the river to see if the girls had crashed, but it was decided that the current was too swift and it wouldn't be safe. The visibility in the water was very poor, so sending down divers wouldn't have achieved anything either. Pam's father would spend days walking up and down the gravel roads and across the nearby fields looking for any signs of the girls. Sherri's father would sit at the local police department looking at photo after photo of unidentified deceased girls, and he checked her social security to see if it was being used by anyone, but it wasn't. The girls had vanished into thin air.

A False Accusation

How a man named David Lykken came to be accused of murdering both Sherri and Pam is quite extraordinary. When questioned, he was already serving 225 years in prison for rape and kidnapping. With no bodies, no forensic evidence, and no witness statements it's hard to believe he was considered for the alleged crime in the first place.

However, Lykken had a very dark history and was in the area of Vermillion at the time the two girls disappeared. The case was handed on to the newly-formed cold case unit in 2004, and was one of the first cases investigated. The fact that Lykken had lived close to the gravel pit where the party was meant to take place that night, and because he had a history of violence towards women, it was deemed he needed to be investigated further.

While going back over the previous records and documents, there was one piece of information gathered back in 1971 that further convinced the investigators to look at Lykken. A neighbor of Pam Jackson's family had reported that she had overheard a party line phone conversation a month before the girls disappeared. It was reportedly a conversation between Pam Jackson and a man named David. The neighbor believed David was a student at the University of South Dakota, but wasn't sure.

They began to question Lykken's victims to try and find out as much information as they could about the crimes he had committed. They also spoke to his younger sister, who claimed he was often violent and threatening. She even recalled an incident in which David told her to drive, and he climbed into the back of the car and raped a female passenger. According to his sister, David had taken the same school bus with Sherri, and he knew both Sherri and Pam through the church.

His sister recalled a time shortly after the disappearances when her family was digging large pits on their farm and creating a large fire. Her parents had often tried to cover for David when he got into trouble, but he still had a lot of anger towards them. The sister didn't know why this was, but she had been told once it was something to do with a girl buried on the farm. At this point in time, she was unaware the cold case team were interviewing her about Sherri and Pam.

Some of the information given by his sister was clearly not true. When asked if she had seen a car on the farm and was shown pictures of different models of Studebaker, she identified the same model Sherri had been driving that night. When asked if she saw any bodies, she claimed she saw Sherri slumped over the steering wheel and Pam with her head on the passenger window. It seemed she was feeding off the suggestions that were given to her instead of recalling actual facts.

With all of the information at hand, the investigators obtained a search warrant for David's possessions that were stored at his parent's farm and for the farmland itself. They dug up many areas as indicated by David's sister on a map, but nothing was found. Numerous other interviews with his sister took place, including under hypnosis, and it seemed as though she was recalling real memories.

In 2006, the investigation team received further information from an inmate named Aloysius Black Crow, who was incarcerated with Lykken. He claimed Lykken had confessed to him that he had murdered Sherri and Pam. They fitted him with a wire and asked him to go back and interview Lykken. He did so, and the audio recording captured Lykken stating he had asked the girls for a ride, and he had raped Pam and tied Sherri up for hours.

It was discovered in 2008 that the tape recordings were all fake, and that it was another man's voice on the tape, not Lykken's. The investigators had been sent down the wrong path—first by Lykken's own sister, then by a fraudulent inmate who was only out to gain for himself. Therefore, the charges against Lykken were dropped.

Skeletons in the Studebaker

In September 2013, the forty-three-year mystery surrounding the disappearance of Sherri Miller and Pam Jackson was finally solved. A fisherman at Brule Creek noticed wheels underneath the bridge while the water levels were low and notified the authorities. On investigation, they discovered that it was the 1960 Studebaker Lark that Sherri had been driving that night.

Inside the car were the skeletal remains of two females who would later be identified as Sherri and Pam. Their identities were confirmed through the use of DNA, and there were a number of personal items found inside the car that belonged to the girls. On examination of the bodies, it was determined that there were no signs of injuries that would indicate foul play or homicide. Instead, the girls had simply run off the road and vanished into the murky depths of the creek.

Despite the area being searched multiple times following the disappearance, the car could not be seen due to higher water levels. Tragically, Pam's father had passed away just five days before the car wreck was discovered. Although it is still a terrible tragedy that the girls were found deceased, it at last puts to rest all of the suspicions, accusations, theories, and what ifs that have plagued the families and the community for nearly fifty years.

CHAPTER 9:
When Suicide is Murder

It's not always easy to tell the difference between a suicide and a murder, and sometimes information comes to light much later on that further clarifies the difference between the two. The case of Pamela Shelly is one such case. At first, it was considered a suicide by the authorities, but thanks to a true crime television program many years later, a man was subsequently caught and put behind bars for her murder.

The Death of Pamela Shelly

Pamela Shelly had been living with her boyfriend Ronnie Hendrick in De Witt County, Texas, not far from where Ronnie's parents lived. Her children Kayla, 12, and Dustin, 9, were also living with Pamela and Ronnie. The rest of her family was back in Arkansas, where she had also been living before Ronnie moved her to Texas. Pamela and her kids had only been at Ronnie's for about five months, and she was planning to leave him. Ronnie was abusive, and Pamela was taking the kids and moving back to Arkansas.

January 6, 2001, Pamela had packed her belongings and sorted the children's things out and was about to leave. They were leaving in twenty minutes time when something happened that would forever change the lives of many. A gunshot was heard, and Pamela was lying on the floor of the bathroom with a bullet wound to the head. Ronnie's stepfather placed the call to 911 asking for assistance because Pamela had attempted to kill herself.

When the ambulance got there, Pamela was still breathing. They quickly loaded her onboard and headed to nearby Cuero, where the hospital was, twenty minutes away. Ronnie was in the front cab of the ambulance giving directions, as the ambulance staff had come from out of town and didn't know their way around. By the time the police arrived at the scene, the ambulance along with Pamela and Ronnie had already left.

Many years later, the emergency services people who attended the incident all stated they must have believed it was a suicide, as there was no fear about entering the house. Usually if there is a firearm incident, the ambulance staff waits at a safe distance until the police clear the scene. This wasn't considered necessary this time and is most likely because the adults that were present all stated Pamela had tried to kill herself.

Ronnie's family made sure the authorities believed Pamela was suicidal. Ronnie claimed that Pamela was happy there, but her daughter Kayla wasn't, and so she had to return to Arkansas even though she didn't want to. Ronnie believed this was the final straw for Pamela, and she took her own life. There was apparently a family history of suicide in Pamela's family, including her sister who had successfully killed herself. Therefore, it's no wonder it seemed so plausible to the investigating officers.

The autopsy performed on Pamela showed a typical suicide gunshot, and adding to that the information given that she was suicidal and depressed, the medical examiner happily labelled the death as a suicide. The police, however, were still uneasy and requested Ronnie take a polygraph, which he agreed to do. They arranged for the test to be done on two separate occasions, but Ronnie failed to appear each time. Weeks after Pamela's death, Ronnie disappeared.

Several years later, in 2008, a new investigator, Carl Bowen, joined the county sheriff's department. The current sheriff was Jody Zavesky, and because Carl had been on the force when Pamela died, he was aware of the case and convinced Jody to take another look at it. Carl had always been bothered by the fact that Ronnie had never taken the polygraph test and had disappeared almost immediately after Pamela died. Fueled by their own determination and personal interest, Jody and Carl reopened the case.

Carl was pleasantly surprised when that summer Ronnie Hendrick was arrested and arrived at the De Witt County Jail. He had been charged with domestic abuse, having beaten up the woman he had been sharing a home with. It turned out that following Pamela's death, Ronnie had traveled to South Dakota and spent time in prison there for felony DWI, as well. All of a sudden, things started to fall into place for Carl as he realized Ronnie was a chronic alcohol abuser and woman beater.

Finally Carl was able to get Ronnie to take the polygraph test. Not surprisingly, he failed it, and when questioned by the polygraph examiner after the test, he requested legal counsel. He told four different people that he had lied about not being in the bathroom when she was shot, but that he did not pull the trigger. Originally he had claimed to be outside the house when Pamela was shot. Things were getting more and more suspicious.

Television Steps In

Carl discovered there was a television program looking for cold cases they could work on and help solve for a new television show called Cold Justice. Although hesitant at first, it was agreed by the higher authorities that the case of Pamela Shelly could be put forward as a possible case for the program. The producers of the show jumped at the chance right away. The main investigators in the program were former Harris County

ADA Kelly Siegler and a former crime scene investigator, Yolanda McClary, from Las Vegas.

The team tends to focus on police departments that are understaffed, where their expertise can be used more effectively. They arrived in June and set to work. With them came the opportunity to have access to high-tech scientific evidence results with a remarkably quick turnaround. Immediately the gun was sent for DNA analysis. Unfortunately, this did not produce the results they wanted or needed.

Next, they took a look at Pamela's medical history and noted there had never been any issue with depression or any other form of mental illness, which completely undermined Ronnie's story. They were able to cross off any information that was no longer relevant or had been disproved, while at the same time gathering new information through witness interviews, crime scene reenactments, and reanalyzing all the previous data that had been gathered. When they presented the case and new evidence, the DA took his time deciding whether or not to proceed.

The final piece of the puzzle that persuaded the DA was an interview conducted by Carl with Pamela's ex-husband Jessie, who was incarcerated in a prison in Texas. According to Jessie, he had a phone conversation the same day Pamela was shot, reconfirming that she and the children were moving back to Arkansas. He also claimed that he and Pam were going to reunite and get back together. During the conversation, Ronnie had grabbed the phone and told Jessie the only way she was going back to Arkansas was in a box. To see if he was being deceptive with his story, Jessie was given a polygraph and passed.

Ronnie Hendrick

In November 2012, Ronnie was indicted for murder. He was set to go to trial in September 2013. Unfortunately, Cold Justice had scheduled the screening of the episode about Pam just six days before the trial was due to begin. Carl contacted the producers and asked if the date could be changed, but they refused. The concern was that if the local people watched the show, they would be useless as a jury. Sure enough, when jury selection came around, so many had seen it and already formed an opinion regarding his guilt that they could not be used as jury members, so a mistrial was called.

Another date was set for the trial, which was to be in June 2014. Although what people had seen on the program may have worn off by then, there was still the chance that a jury could be difficult to select. The DA decided to use that to his advantage and had a meeting with Ronnie's attorney. When it was pointed out that every person who had watched the Cold Justice episode was likely to believe Ronnie was guilty, then the jury was going to be the same. Therefore, it was likely he would be found guilty even if a jury could be selected. The next day, Ronnie pled guilty to murder and was sentenced to twenty-two years in prison.

CHAPTER 10:
Snatched From the Snow

The story of Maria Ridulph is a tragic tale and one of innocence lost that would affect not only her family, but her community. It would also greatly affect a friend, who had been with her that night and witnessed the abduction, for the rest of her life. Two little girls innocently playing in the snow outside the house were ripped apart by a real life boogeyman who swept in and swept out, carrying little Maria away with him.

The Disappearance of Maria Ridulph

Maria was one of four children born to parents Michael and Frances, and they lived in Sycamore, Illinois. Most of the adults in the area worked on local farms, but Michael worked at a factory, one of the few that existed there at that time. Frances was a homemaker, taking care of the family and the home, and they seemed to have a good life.

It had started snowing on the evening of December 3, 1957, and Maria begged her parents to let her go out and play in the snow with her friend Kathy Sigman. Although it was dark out, her parents said yes, and after dinner they went outside near

Maria's home and were playing a game they called 'duck the cars', where they ran back and forth avoiding the headlights of cars coming down the street. In that era it wasn't considered dangerous to let the kids out at night, as it was a fairly innocent time, a time when murders and violent crimes were not common at all.

While they were out playing, Kathy stated a man had approached them who said his name was Johnny. He told them he was twenty-four years old and had no wife, and he offered Maria a piggyback ride. She went back to her house and retrieved her favorite doll to show the stranger, as it was her prized possession. When she returned, Kathy went back to her own house to get her mittens because it was so cold. When Kathy came back, both Maria and the stranger were gone.

Unable to find Maria, Kathy went to her parent's house to tell them she couldn't find her. Maria's parents assumed she was hiding somewhere and sent their 11-year-old son out to find her. When he had no luck, the parents then called the police. Within an hour, the police had arrived along with armed civilians to search the town. They could find no trace of the little girl or the man who she had last been seen with.

Within two days of her disappearance, the FBI was called in due to the possibility Maria had been kidnapped and taken across state lines. Numerous people had seen the two girls playing together that night, but nobody had seen the stranger with them up until 6:30 p.m. They therefore believed this stranger, 'Johnny', had approached Maria and Kathy after that time, and that Maria had been taken somewhere between 6:45 and 7:00 p.m.

Because Kathy had been the only one to see Johnny, she was placed in protective custody in case he returned to take her or harm her. She was shown photos of possible suspects or those who had been convicted before to see if she could identify the man who called himself Johnny, but she could not. She was also asked to look at a lineup of suspects, and she pointed out a man named Thomas Joseph Rivard. However, Rivard had a tight alibi and couldn't have been the man they were looking for. He had only been placed in the lineup to fill up the numbers.

A Tragic Discovery

Near Woodbine, Illinois, some 100 miles away from Sycamore, two tourists were searching a wooded area looking for mushrooms on April 26, 1958. What they found was the skeletal remains of a young child. The only clothing present was a shirt, socks, and undershirt, and the tiny body was beneath a tree that had partially fallen over. The state of decomposition indicated the body had been there for months, and it was later identified as Maria through dental records. The rest of the clothing she had been wearing the night she disappeared was nowhere to be seen.

Photographs of the crime scene were not taken, as the coroner didn't want the media to get hold of them, particularly because the body was that of a child. As the body was found within the state, the FBI stepped back and left the case with the local and state police to investigate. The autopsy done at the time showed no indication of the manner of death. This was apparently due to the level of decomposition, which many years later would be handled in a different manner.

Prime Suspect Right From the Start – Was Tessier Johnny?

A young man who was considered a suspect right from the beginning was John Tessier. Originally from Ireland, he had moved to Sycamore after World War II ended with his British mother and American stepfather. Before his mother's remarriage, John's surname had been Cherry, and he would still use it from time to time.

The family home was just around the corner from the Ridulph's, and at the time John was eighteen years old and planning on joining the Air Force. During the initial search and investigation into Maria's disappearance, investigators had visited John's home and spoken to his mother. She claimed John had been home all night, whereas his sisters would later testify this wasn't true. The investigators had received a tip regarding John, and it was speculated that it may have come from a resident or John's parents themselves, trying to clear their boy's name since he had the same name as Johnny and his physical description was a match.

The next statement John made was that he had been in Rockford the night in question enlisting in the Air Force, which completely contradicted what his mother had said previously. He claimed he had called his parents from Rockford to get a ride home, as he had left his car back at the house. There was a telephone record of a collect call being made that night at 6:57 p.m. by a John Tessier. He then met with recruiting officers to drop off some paperwork, and they confirmed to the authorities that this occurred at around 7:15 p.m. that night.

Despite this, an officer wasn't convinced and asked Tessier to take a polygraph test, which he complied with and passed. Because his alibi seemed to be truthful and he had passed the polygraph, he was released and taken off the list of suspects. Of note, Kathy Sigman was never asked to identify John or look at his photograph. The following day, John left for training at the Air Force Base.

John was to complete thirteen years in the Air Force, and he obtained the rank of captain before then undertaking study to become a police officer. He worked as an officer in Lacy, Olympia, then moved to Milton, Washington. Trouble would find him in Washington in 1982 in the form of a 15-year-old runaway named Michelle Weinman and her friend. John had taken the girls in, and not long after, Michelle filed a complaint that John had fondled her and performed oral sex. He was charged with felony statutory rape and discharged from the police force. He negotiated a plea deal and pled guilty to communication with a minor for immoral purposes, which is a misdemeanor instead of a felony. John would later change his name to Jack Daniel McCullough, supposedly to honor his deceased mother.

A Mother's Deathbed Confession

In 2008, John Tessier's half-sister Janet provided new information that led to the case being reopened. She made a startling revelation that on her mother's deathbed she had stated the following: "Those two little girls, and the one that disappeared, John did it. John did it and you have to tell someone." Janet immediately assumed her mother was talking about the murder of Maria Ridulph and had been told by her elder sisters that their mother had lied to the police that night about John's whereabouts. Another of the half-sisters, Mary, was also there when their mother made the statement about John being guilty, but she only heard the words 'he did it'. Nevertheless, she also assumed it was to do with the Maria Ridulph case. At the time of their mother's death, John was not involved in the family, having previously molested a younger half-sister and threatened Janet with a gun. He wasn't even allowed to come to his mother's funeral.

Janet had made numerous attempts since her mother's death to get the Sycamore police and the FBI to consider her mother's statement. She eventually sent an email to the Illinois State Police tip line, and it was handed to the cold case unit to investigate. All of John's sisters had suspected him of being the murderer. The investigators were able to create a different timeline showing that John did have time to drive to Rockford after snatching Maria and making the phone call to his parents and meeting with the recruitment officers. This shed a whole new light on his so-called alibi.

Finally, Kathy Sigman, Maria's friend who had been there that dreadful night, was shown a photograph of John as he was back then. She immediately identified him as the stranger, 'Johnny', who had disappeared with Maria. More and more evidence was stacking up against John, as witnesses recalled new information and other witnesses came forward. In 2011, John was asked to come in to the police station to answer some questions. Whenever he was asked about that night or Maria Ridulph he would become aggressive and evasive with his answers. He refused to answer any further questions and was subsequently arrested for the abduction and murder of Maria.

The same month, Maria's tiny body was exhumed and tested for DNA evidence with no luck. A forensic anthropologist examined the skeleton and was able to determine she had been stabbed in the throat with a long blade at least three times. Although this was most likely the cause of death, other causes couldn't be ruled out due to the lack of soft tissue, with which other injuries such as strangulation may have been identified. Nevertheless, the case was pursued and a trial set.

A Long-Awaited Trial

John went to trial in September 2012 for the murder of Maria. Evidence and testimonies were heard from those who had been involved in the case, as well as from some inmates who claimed John had confessed to the murder while awaiting trial. One claimed John said he strangled her with a wire, while another claimed John said he smothered her accidentally while trying to stop her from screaming. On September 14, he was found guilty of the abduction and murder of Maria and was given a life sentence. A parole period of twenty years was given, however, John was seventy-three years of age at the time of the sentencing.

John filed a petition for post-conviction relief in 2015, and after extensive investigation by the state's Attorney, it was determined that he was innocent. A court hearing took place in March 2016 and the conviction was overturned. The dismissal of the charge of murder was without prejudice, which means that another charge of murder of Maria Ridulph could be brought against him in the future.

CHAPTER 11:
Captive for 24 Years – the Joseph Fritzl Case

This case takes place in a town called Amstetten in Austria, when it was discovered a man had kept his daughter captive for twenty-four years in the basement of the family home. She had been abused, raped, and assaulted, and would not be free until she was forty-two years of age and had birthed seven children by her father. For a daughter to be treated so heinously by a man who is supposed to love and protect her is abominable and that the children they created suffered such psychological damage is horrendous. This man and his wife were the epitome of evil.

An Incestuous Situation

Joseph Fritzl and his wife Rosemarie had a large family, comprised of seven children. There were five daughters and two sons. Elisabeth was born in 1966, and her father began to abuse her from the time she was eleven years old. She went on to complete the required education, and at fifteen she undertook study on waitressing. Elisabeth ran away from home in January 1983 and fled to Vienna with a work friend. The police were notified, and she was found and returned to her parents. Reluctantly, she had to go back, but she did finish her course and was offered a job.

When Elisabeth was eighteen, her father told her he needed help carrying a door down into the basement of the home. She agreed to help and even held the door in place while he attached it to the frame. Little did she know that it was this door that would keep her locked inside. Josef then held a towel soaked in ether over her face, and once she was unconscious, he locked her in the basement.

Following her disappearance, her mother filed a missing person report with the authorities. Josef then began forcing Elisabeth to write letters saying she no longer wanted to live with her family and she had moved away with her friend. One letter stated that if they came looking for her she would flee the country. Josef had also told the authorities that he believed she had joined a religious cult. All of this was nonsense, of course, as she was in the basement of the family home the whole time.

Elisabeth was repeatedly raped by Josef during the twenty-four years he held her captive. She gave birth to seven children without any medical treatment whatsoever. One baby died just after he was born, and three of them were sent upstairs to live with Josef and Rosemarie. They told social services that the children had just appeared on the doorstep, and they were left in their care by the authorities with regular checkups. At no time was there any suspicion by social services as to what was really going on.

After the birth of the fourth child, Josef enlarged the captivity area so that Elisabeth had more space for herself and her children. Instead of bringing her food every few days, she now had a refrigerator to store food in, as well as hotplates to heat the meals up. They now had a radio, a television, and a video player to entertain them. Elisabeth spent her time teaching her children basic schooling, such as how to read and write. If Josef felt they needed punishing, he would switch off their light supply or refuse to bring them food for days at a time. Elisabeth was told by Josef that if they tried to escape, they would all be gassed.

A Visit to the Hospital Invokes Suspicion

The eldest daughter of Elisabeth and Josef, Kerstin, was unwell and fell unconscious on April 19, 2008. Josef agreed to seek medical care for Kerstin, and Elisabeth helped him carry her upstairs. It was the first time Elisabeth had been out of the basement for twenty-four years. She was ushered back to the basement, and Kerstin was sent by ambulance to the hospital. Josef arrived later and said he had found a note by Elisabeth. The staff at the hospital found this very strange and alerted law enforcement on April 21. They made a media appeal for Elisabeth to come forward, and at the same time reopened her missing person's case. Again, Josef reiterated his beliefs that she had joined a cult and produced another letter from January 2008 as the most recent one he had received. It was found that the postmark on the letter was not an area known for cults, and the way the letters were written seemed as though they had been dictated.

Elisabeth was desperate to see Kerstin, and Josef finally agreed on April 26. Once at the hospital, the doctor taking care of Kerstin alerted the police that they were there, and they were subsequently detained and taken to the station for questioning. Elisabeth wouldn't say anything until the police promised her that she would never have to see Josef ever again. She then proceeded to tell them in great detail of her ordeal in the basement and all the horrific things Josef had made her do. Following her statement, Josef was immediately arrested under suspicion of serious crimes committed against family members.

The Trial of Josef Fritzl

Josef's trial was perhaps one of the shortest in history, lasting just four days. He had pled guilty to all charges, included rape, incest, coercion, enslavement, false imprisonment, and the negligent homicide of the baby, Michael, who died shortly after birth due to lack of medical care. He was ultimately sentenced to life imprisonment, while Elisabeth, her children, and her mother were all taken into care. Throughout the trial, more was learnt about the background of Josef. He had a long history of violent crime, including rape and attempted rape. He was also known for indecently exposing himself. Although he had once been incarcerated, the conviction was expunged after a period of fifteen years, so when social services became involved, his background check did not reveal his previous crimes.

The Psychological Scars and Fighting Back to Normality

Following their arrival into care, Elisabeth, the children, and her mother were placed in a clinic where they could receive all the medical and psychological treatment they might need. They were shielded from the prying outside world as they grasped the enormity of what they were going through. The three children who had been kept in the basement and even Elisabeth needed therapy to adjust to natural light after being kept in a semi-dark space for so long. It was also difficult to adjust to having space to move around in.

All were plagued with panic attacks and anxiety. One child was unable to walk properly due to having to stoop for so long in the basement. Another tore her hair out and stuffed her clothing into the toilet. The children that had been kept upstairs had issues with resentment and anger. The treatment and therapy for Elisabeth and her children will be an ongoing need for many years to come.

CHAPTER 12:
A Controversial Case of Police Misconduct – Or Was it Murder By Cop?

Nizah Morris was an entertainer who also happened to be transgender. She had been living as a female since her early 20s, and her day job was working for her mother at her daycare center. At night she would perform in a drag show at a bar called Bob and Barbara's in Philadelphia's Center City. She was also a practicing Buddhist, calm by nature and making a good life for herself. Tragically, all that came to an end on December 22, 2002. The controversy that followed would rock the legal system and create support from all walks of life for the rights of transgender people.

Nizah Morris Left Lying in the Street

Nizah had been to a party at a bar located at the intersection of Chancellor and Juniper streets in Philadelphia. The bar was called the Key West Bar, and she reportedly left at around 2 a.m. On exiting the bar, Nizah collapsed on the ground outside, intoxicated. Those who were outside the bar formed a group around her and alerted the paramedics. Nizah was unable to even stand unsupported at this point.

An officer from the 6th District police precinct arrived, and because Nizah refused to go to hospital the ambulance was cancelled. Instead, the police officer offered her a ride to the hospital, but she declined this also. All Nizah wanted to do was go home. Those who were nearby helped Nizah into the police car, and the officers proceeded to take her home. Her address was in the 5000 block of Walnut Street, but the officers claimed she wanted to be let out of the car at 15th and Walnut streets. They noticed her walking towards 16th Street.

Just minutes later, a motorist driving by saw Nizah lying on the sidewalk. She had an injury on the side of her forehead that was bleeding, and a call was made to 911 asking for medical assistant. This time an officer for the 9th District precinct arrived. A call was not made to a supervisor, and the situation was not considered nor treated as a crime.

By the time Nizah arrived at hospital, her condition was critical. Life support was removed on December 23 and she was pronounced dead on December 24 at 8:30 p.m. The medical examiner ruled the death as a homicide on December 25, but the police department's homicide unit would not accept it. They instead classified it as an accidental death. A second opinion was then requested.

Police Request a Second Opinion

The controversy surrounding this case was whether or not the police officers acted appropriately in their interactions with Nizah that night. For starters, even though she was refusing medical treatment in the first instance, the ambulance should not have been cancelled. Also, even though the police officers were not required to drive her home, once they had agreed to do so, they were responsible for getting her home safe and sound. They certainly shouldn't have dropped her off elsewhere and let her walk off when earlier she couldn't even stand unaided due to her level of intoxication. If it was only minutes later that she was found injured on the sidewalk; the officers couldn't have been watching her walk away safely.

The family, friends, and the community in general had many questions regarding what happened to Nizah that night. It would be easy to assume it was an accident—she was drunk and quite easily could have fallen and whacked her head. But, the medical examiner called it a homicide. So who was the perpetrator? Was there an assailant or was it homicide by negligence and failure to provide due care?

According to Nizah's family members, the photographs they were shown at the medical examiner's office showed marks on her wrists like indentations, as well as what appeared to be defensive wounds on her hands. The local newspaper ran a story on the tragedy on December 31, but they abhorrently referred to Nizah as a prostitute and a male. This further fueled the fires that were already burning among her family and friends. She was cremated on January 1, 2003, with more than 300 people attending the service.

A second opinion was sought from a brain injury specialist. The tests undertaken showed that she had died due to a cerebral injury, otherwise known as a brain injury. On January 30, the homicide division declared the case a homicide.

There were numerous inconsistencies in the police reports from that night in relation to witness statements. Protests were being held due to the handling of the case by the police department. There were issues surrounding Nizah not being identified for nearly 64 hours while she was in the hospital, despite her fingerprints being on record. One of the officers present actually knew Nizah, but he did not identify her either. Those who had been at the scene also told the police officers who Nizah was, but this information was never passed on either.

There were too many questions and not enough answers, and the community was rallying for further investigation. In April 2003, the District Attorney launched an investigation into the case, but it would be short-lived and provided no answers at all, just more questions.

The Investigation into the Officers

The investigation started by the District Attorney quickly ended in December, failing to find who was responsible for Nizah's death. The DA appealed to the public for help, and declared at the same time that the three police officers involved in the incident had all acted appropriately. Complaints were lodged by Nizah's mother against the police department for not providing all of the information to the family. A civil suit was brought against the bar that allowed Nizah to become intoxicated, as well as the officers involved, the EMTs, and the city of Philadelphia, by the Center for Lesbian and Gay Civil Rights. Interestingly this suit was settled in May 2004 for $250,000.

Police Advisory Commission Called In

An initial investigation undertaken by the Police Advisory Commission asserting that the only officer who hadn't acted properly that night was an Officer Skala. The Philadelphia Police Department advised the Commission within days that they had not received all of the documentation, as some of it was missing, including the homicide report, which had been missing since 2003. As a side note, this report miraculously reappeared in 2011 in the archives.

The Commission voted to reopen the investigation in March 2008. This investigation proved to be fruitless and pointless, so the initial findings remained standing. Once again they voted to reinvestigate in 2011, and at the end of the investigation they called for the U.S. Attorney General's Office to fully investigate the case. They in turn, declined. By 2015, the only result from all of the investigations was that Officer Skala received a verbal reprimand, even though it was found that she had lied and deliberately deceived the department about her interactions with Nizah that night. She eventually ended up working in the commissioner's office—what a punishment! No wonder so many people lost their faith in the Philadelphia legal system.

Something Good from Something Bad

In honor of Nizah, Philadelphia opened a center for drug addiction treatment for transgender persons. The official name is 'The Morris Home for Trans and Gender-Variant People'. To date it is the only inpatient center of its kind that is run by transgender people for transgender people. Nizah may have lost her life, but in her name she is helping others to save theirs.

GET ONE OF MY AUDIOBOOKS FOR FREE

audible
an amazon company

If you haven't joined Audible yet, you can get any of my audiobooks for FREE!
Go to www.JackRosewood.com to find out how!

More books by Jack Rosewood

The world can be a very strange place in general and when you open the pages of this true crime anthology you will quickly learn that the criminal world specifically can be as bizarre as it is dangerous. In the following book, you will be captivated by mysterious missing person cases that defy all logic and a couple cases of murderous mistaken identity. Follow along as detectives conduct criminal investigations in order to solve cases that were once believed to be unsolvable. Every one of the crime cases chronicled in the pages of this book are as strange and disturbing as the next.

The twelve true crime stories in this book will keep you riveted as you turn the pages, but they will probably also leave you with more questions than answers. For instance, you will be left pondering how two brothers from the same family could disappear with no trace in similar circumstances over ten years apart. You will also wonder how two women with the same first and last names, but with no personal connections, could be murdered within the same week in the same city. The examination of a number of true crime murder cases that went cold, but were later solved through scientific advances, will also keep you intrigued and reading.

Open the pages of this book, if you dare, to read some of the most bizarre cases of disappearances, mistaken identity, and true murder. Some of the cases will disturb and anger you, but make no mistake, you will want to keep reading!

Of all the many psychopaths and sociopaths that have hunted for human victims throughout history, few have been more disturbing or mysterious than Christopher Bernard Wilder – the beauty queen killer. From the middle of the 1960s until 1984, Wilder sexually assaulted countless women and murdered at least nine in Australia and the United States. The beauty queen killer was not only a true psychopath, but also a hunter as he carefully chose attractive girls and young women to victimize. But Wilder was no creepy looking killer; he was an attractive, articulate man who used a camera and offers of a modelling career to get his unsuspecting, naïve victims to remote locations where he would then rape, torture, and ultimately kill them.

Among serial killer biographies, Wilder's is a cautionary tale. First as a juvenile and later as a young man, Wilder was arrested on numerous occasions for sexual assaults in both

Australia and United States; but he never served any time behind bars due to technicalities, witnesses refusing to testify, or the judges showing sympathy towards the beauty queen killer. When one considers some of the better known American crime stories from history, many red-flags are apparent that point towards the future criminal potential of an individual: for Wilder, the flags were bright, crimson, quite large, and difficult to avoid, yet were ignored by his friends, family, and the authorities. Christopher Wilder's saga is therefore not just a true crime murder story, but also an unfortunate example of how the system can fail to protect the public from a known sexual sadist.

Open the pages of this intriguing book and read the story of an American serial killer who had it all: looks, money, and beautiful women. But as this captivating true crime story will reveal, nothing was ever enough for the beauty queen killer as he killed his way across the United States in order to satisfy his sadistic lust. Aspects of the Christopher Bernard Wilder story will disturb you, but at the same time you will find it difficult to put this serial killer biography down because you will be drawn in by the FBI's hunt to capture the elusive criminal.

Richmond, Virginia: On the morning of October 19, 1979, parolee James Briley stood before a judge and vowed to quit the criminal life. That same day, James met with brothers Linwood, Anthony, and 16-year-old neighbor Duncan Meekins. What they planned—and carried out—would make them American serial-killer legends, and reveal to police investigators a 7-month rampage of rape, robbery, and murder exceeding in brutality already documented cases of psychopaths, sociopaths, and sex criminals.

As reported in this book, the Briley gang were responsible for the killing of 11 people (among these, a 5-year-old boy and his pregnant mother), but possibly as many as 20. Unlike most criminals, however, the Briley gang's break-ins and robberies were purely incidental—mere excuses for rape and vicious thrill-kills. When authorities (aided by plea-bargaining Duncan Meekins) discovered the whole truth, even their tough skins crawled. Nothing in Virginian history approached the depravities, many of which were committed within miles of the Briley home, where single father James Sr. padlocked himself into his bedroom every night.

But this true crime story did not end with the arrests and murder convictions of the Briley gang. Linwood, younger brother James, and 6 other Mecklenburg death-row inmates, hatched an incredible plan of trickery and manipulation—and escaped from the "state-of-the-art" facility on May 31, 1984. The biggest death-row break-out in American history.

GET THESE BOOKS FOR FREE

Go to www.jackrosewood.com
and get these E-Books for free!

A Note From The Author

Hello, this is Jack Rosewood. Thank you for reading this book. I hope you enjoyed the read. If you did, I'd appreciate if you would take a few moments to post a review on Amazon.

I would also love if you'd sign up to my newsletter to receive updates on new releases, promotions and a FREE copy of my Herbert Mullin E-Book, go to www.JackRosewood.com

Thanks again for reading this book, make sure to follow me on Facebook.

Best Regards

Jack Rosewood